P9-DWJ-365

WARNING

LIBERALISM IS A MENTAL DISORDER
CONTAINS ADULT LANGUAGE,
ADULT CONTENT, PSYCHOLOGICAL NUDITY

READER DISCRETION ADVISED

LIBERALISM
IS A MENTAL DISORDER

LIBERALISM
IS A MENTAL DISORDER

Savage Solutions

MICHAEL
SAVAGE

NELSON CURRENT
A Subsidiary of Thomas Nelson, Inc.

Published in Nashville, Tennessee, by Nelson Current, a division of a wholly-owned subsidiary (Nelson Communications, Inc.) of Thomas Nelson, Inc.

Nelson Current books may be purchased in bulk for educational, business, fundraising, or sales promotional use. For information, please e-mail SpecialMarkets@ThomasNelson.com.

Library of Congress Cataloging-in-Publication Data

Savage, Michael.
    Liberalism is a mental disorder : Savage solutions / Michael Savage.
        p. cm.
    Includes bibliographical references.
    ISBN 978-1-59555-006-4 (hard cover)
    ISBN 978-1-59555-043-9 (trade paper)
    1. United States—Politics and governments—2001– 2. Liberalism—United
States. 3. Conservatism—United States. I. Title.
    JK421.S29   2005
    320.51'3'0973—dc22   2005003063

Printed in the United States of America
06 07 08 09 10 RRD 5 4 3 2 1

TO THE AMERICAN SOLDIER

CONTENTS

PREFACE

The conservative movement is dead. I take no pleasure in making that observation. Let's face facts. Most of the red-state politicians fail to comprehend that the American people are behind them and that the people want them to push through Congress a real conservative agenda. I wish that these empty suits and skirts would provide the leadership necessary to defend America from those who would do her harm instead of taking the side of the enemy!

Can you think of one speech wherein the Republican leadership has expressed a desire to protect our borders, our language, or our culture? Without those three fundamental pillars of society, no nation can survive. Except for a few minor utterances about cultural issues with little or no follow-up, there has been scant support for these conservative principles or values.

On my radio show over the last decade, people have repeatedly called expressing their fears that our national sovereignty is diminishing and that this country will be sold out to an international New World Order. They fear that American citizens will no longer have the protections of our U.S. Constitution. That it will be replaced by a Constitution forged by the

United Nations. No longer will we have the Bill of Rights to protect us; it will be a new, watered-down bill of wrongs from the new, ruling bureaucrats. The concern that American law will be subjected to international law is not an empty fear. Case in point.

In January of 2005, the Mexican government meddled with an Arizona state law, Proposition 200, which had been passed overwhelmingly by the voters of Arizona. This measure mandated three things: It required proof of citizenship to vote in Arizona elections; it denied illegal aliens from receiving taxpayer benefits; and it instructed state employees who discover ineligible applicants to report violators to the authorities. As a border state with a severe illegal alien problem—primarily from Mexico—Arizonans took reasonable measures to defend themselves from illegals who were exploiting the system. Even 40 percent of Mexican Americans in Arizona voted yes on 200!

The reaction south of the border was criminal and terroristic! The Mexican government was so angered by Arizona's attempt to restrict public benefits and deny voting privileges for non-U.S. citizens, Mexico threatened legal action against America! Foreign Secretary Luis Ernesto whined, "We are seeking all the legal opportunities that exist, first using the legal capacities of the United States itself and . . . if that does not work, bringing it to international tribunals."[1]

Who gave Mexico the right to dictate American policy?

Frankly, Mexico doesn't have a Chihuahua in this fight. Last time I checked, Arizona was not a Mexican territory, nor can Mexico require us to put illegal Mexican aliens on the dole. That hasn't stopped the Mexican American Legal Defense and Education Fund—a *bona fide* enemy within—from lecturing us, saying that Proposition 200 is "an illegal, impermissible, unconstitutional state attempt to regulate immigration policy, which is a fundamental function and responsibility of our federal government. Proposition 200 is mean-spirited and un-American."[2]

Worse, our federal officials seem to be allies of those international forces who would override our democracy. Why hasn't there been one statement from the State Department backing the right of Arizona's citizens to do their part to protect our borders and our sovereignty? Where is the outrage from the White House when Mexico threatens legal action against one of our states?

I believe the only thing that can save America is a new appreciation of her national identity. Oliver Wendell Holmes Jr. once wrote, "As life is action and passion, it is required of a man that he should share the passion and action of his time, at the peril of being not to have lived." Taking that a step further, if we fail to act and to pursue a new American nationalism, we will fail to exist as a nation.

> THESE EURO-SOCIALISTS AND THEIR AMERICAN COUNTERPARTS SEE A TERRIBLE BEAUTY STRUGGLING TO BE BORN, A BEAUTY THAT WOULD LIKE TO SWEEP AWAY OUR DYING CIVILIZATION AND BRING US INTO AN UNBRAVE NEW WORLD.

The emergence of an international social liberalism, which is at its core soft-communism, is a very real threat to the sovereignty of our nation. Forces from within and without our country continue to try to tell us that we are out of step with the rest of the world. The "sophisticated" Europeans laugh at us for our naïveté and our clinging to religion and family values. These Euro-socialists and their American counterparts see a terrible beauty struggling to be born, a beauty that would like to sweep away our dying civilization and bring us into an unbrave new world.

Their guilt over their material comforts has not diminished their willingness to fight for a twelve-week vacation every year, to dine at the top of the food chain on a regular basis, nor to enjoy all of the other pleasures of materialism, yet they would have us believe that the many gifts of America were stolen and that *we,* in the socialist tradition, must "redistribute" our wealth, taking from the rich and giving to the poor.

The latest of these socialist scams has been trumpeted by French President Jacques Chirac. In January 2005 Jacques, strapped for new ways to extract cash from Americans and itching to repair his image in the world community, proposed a global tax to advance AIDS research. He envisioned taxing international financial transactions under the guise of providing education and medication for HIV/AIDS patients. In all probability, his proposal would be about as successful as the corrupt United Nations oil-for-food program. Not to mention that I've already paid for AIDS for the past twenty-five years: local, state, and federal taxes, increased health-care costs, increased welfare costs—are all tied to the AIDS pandemic.

These concepts are straight out of the *New Communist Manifesto* wrapped in the rhetoric of justice and fairness. Our children are being inculcated with the international-socialist credos from crib to college. They are being taught that European socialist leaders are men of superior brains who must triumph over the ignorance, the stupidity, and the shortsighted selfishness of the American masses.

Couched under the phrase "for the common good" they are rapidly trying to move us out of our Constitution and into the handcuffs of an emerging New Age. Have you heard this warning from our Republican leadership? Do you hear these words at conservative think tanks?

No.

Rarely, if ever, are these ideas discussed.

What used to be a conservative movement has become nothing more than a series of writings and speeches devoted to attacking the Democratic Party. Even the so-called publications of America's "right wing" such as the

Weekly Standard are little more than support props of the Republicans. Which is why a new nationalism must arise out of the ashes of conservatism.

A few of the impediments standing in the way of a new American nationalism include the inherent fear that such nationalism is intimately tied to Christian doctrine, or, worse, inherently racist. While it is true that some of the better principles of our Constitution and the Bill of Rights are derived directly from the Bible, it must be remembered that the Bible derives from Abraham, the father of the Jewish people, and that the New Testament derives from the Old Testament. So when the internationalists attack Christian fundamentalism, let us not forget they are also attacking Judaism.

While secularists are very sensitive about attacking Judaism and go out of their way to avoid appearing to do so, they—like Adolf Hitler who went before them—have no such qualms when attacking Christianity. Hitler wanted National Socialism imposed as a new global religion and viewed Christianity as a hindrance to his plans. He concluded that he had to first abolish Christianity if he were to succeed with his new state religion, paganism plus a racist socialism. During World War II, Hitler instituted "Operation Rabat" in which he directly ordered one of his generals to kidnap Pope Pius XII. While the general refused to comply with Hitler's wishes, the incident demonstrates the extreme measures socialists are willing to undertake to have their radical agenda executed.[3]

> WHEN THE INTERNATIONALISTS ATTACK CHRISTIAN FUNDAMENTALISM, LET US NOT FORGET THEY ARE ALSO ATTACKING JUDAISM.

In this book, I have exposed these insanities and inanities of extreme leftist thought; those actions and policies which have greatly undermined our moral heritage and foundational beliefs. As I've demonstrated, the very glory of America is being erased in our lifetime. Consider this: How many Americans still know what flag they live under? Is it the stars and stripes?

The UN flag?

The rainbow flag?

The Mexican flag?

The red flag or the blue flag?

Each of the above are now equally displayed in too many places across our country. A strong conservative leadership would prohibit this blurring of banners and would prohibit the use of anything but the English language in official discourse or in the application for government benefits or voting. What nation can hold together when their ballots are printed in many languages (as is the case in San Francisco and elsewhere)?

While the left is marshalling their battalions to assault the pillars of America, the right is disorganized and provides little national leadership. How, then, can we defend our borders, language, and culture from the neo-Marxist left? One of the best weapons we have to save America's sovereignty is to expose our enemies by mocking our enemies. To this end, humor is a great weapon. Why?

Ultimately, the legions of leftist revolutionaries are laughable. Their ideology has been a complete failure wherever it has been tried. Unfortunately, they are taken too seriously. Which is why I invite you to sneer at their Big Lie. I invite you to remain vigilant before a bomb goes off in your mother's house.

THIS BOOK HAS BEEN DESIGNED TO POUR A CAUSTIC SOLUTION ON THE EDIFICES OF LIBERALISM.

My first book in this trilogy, *The Savage Nation,* was a call to action. My second book, *The Enemy Within,* alerted the reader to the very real domestic traitors. This book has been designed to pour a caustic solution on the edifices of liberalism, using their own actions and policies as the dissolving solutions.

INTRODUCTION

In this book I will demonstrate how well-intentioned liberal programs, plans, and ideas often lead to terrible results. While the impulse for helping others is well intentioned, the results often border on insanity.

As such, is liberalism a mental disorder?

Can all liberals be mentally disordered? Are good intentions good enough? Let me define the terms. By liberalism and liberals I do not refer to, nor do I condemn, those who wish to help their fellow man of lesser fortune. However, it is on the fringes of compassion and the jagged border of anarchy to want to erase our borders, our language, and our culture.

I realize some will be tempted to dismiss words like "liberal" and "conservative," even the word "fascist," as unenlightened, hackneyed terms. Yet, as you will see, liberalism and her committed foot soldiers do very much exist. Their twisted logic and their revolutionary zeal continue to plague America and her institutions. This is a book, then, about liberal believers and the consequences of their beliefs.

Granted, true Democrats, the so-called blue-America, probably consider themselves just as patriotic (if not more so) than the residents of so-called red-America (the Republicans). But in their zeal to help the unfortunate, they are now largely espousing the tenets of socialism, not democracy. By wanting to take from the haves and give to the have-nots they assume that all Americans who *have* got that way by ill-gotten means, while all who have-not are both deserving of their generosity and have somehow been cheated of their own rightful place in society.

Moreover, as they are pulled farther in by the fringe soothsayers and the Pied Pipers of the Democrat Party, they become gulled into believing in the lessening or dissolution of America's sovereignty and in embracing an allegiance to "European" (i.e. socialist) concepts. The "World Court" and the "United Nations" have become their touchstones, replacing the United States Constitution and the Bill of Rights. "Big" corporations are seen as exploitive giants to be slain, while a one-world, global government is accepted as a necessarily benign and compassionate entity.

> AS THEY ARE PULLED FARTHER IN BY THE FRINGE SOOTHSAYERS AND THE PIED PIPERS OF THE DEMOCRAT PARTY, THEY BECOME GULLED INTO BELIEVING IN THE LESSENING OR DISSOLUTION OF AMERICA'S SOVEREIGNTY AND IN EMBRACING AN ALLEGIANCE TO "EUROPEAN" (I.E. SOCIALIST) CONCEPTS.

The disorder of liberalism has so twisted reality that the traditional family is called "dysfunctional" while the "community" is regarded as the hope of mankind; the priests are reviled while the imams are revered; the cops are arrested for arresting illegal immigrants; the ACLU sues the Boy Scouts and defends the boy lovers; the terrorists are tolerated when they should be annihilated; while Arafat, Kinsey, and Clinton are glorified when they should be vilified.

These are the unintended consequences of liberalism.

In an attempt to do good, very often very bad things happen. Take, for example, gay marriage. Even the straights who reluctantly support this mockery of mankind's most fundamental institution will admit that the unintended consequence of their benevolence may be the dissolution of the institution of marriage itself. By seeking to bestow "equality" on all institutions (when absolute equality cannot exist) they may actually destroy that which they are trying to extend to others.

How is marriage destroyed by granting the right to this sacred institution to homosexuals? By completely rendering marriage meaningless.

Although the impulse is to "do good" by expanding the institution of marriage to include all, the actual result is to devalue the institution itself. Americans in the red states knew this, which is why they voted for a president who promised to defend the institution of marriage. And voters in eleven states overwhelming voted for bans on gay marriage.

Indeed, a host of lessons about the disorder of liberalism can be drawn from the election of 2004.

OFF THE BEATEN TRACK

Various socialist agendas attached themselves to the Democratic train, and slowly but surely Marxism became its engine. Camouflaged under a number of different catchphrases, what was once a caboose had become the engine, an engine that drove the DNC train off the cliff.

Cars in the Democrat train included the anti-war car filled with disgruntled, street crazies from the 1960s who had now become professors and back-room media personalities. This pacifist (i.e. Marxist-Leninist) car clamored for attention throughout the election while our young men were fighting and dying in Iraq trying to keep Islamofascism from our shores. The disloyal internationalists were running up the white flag of surrender under the guise of peace. The American people intuitively knew this and voted down the pretentious "War Hero," John Kerry.

Another car on the train of disaster for the Democrats was the universal health-care car. How many times did we hear the chant, *Health care! Health care! Health care!* coming out of John Kerry's and Edwards's mouth? I knew it wasn't a big issue in America. I knew most Americans, while somewhat concerned, did not put it as a top priority. And yet the out-of-touch Democrats kept harping on this. Post-election analysis revealed just 8 percent of voters considered health care when placing their vote. Just 8 percent!

To further demonstrate how out of touch the left wing is in this country, during a subsequent post-election analysis, a group of saddened Democrat "leaders" were analyzing what had happened. One of them from the Democrat Leadership Counsel—one of the same village idiots who pushed Bill Clinton over the finish line—said, "I believe in order to remain a viable party we've got to emphasize the environment in future elections."

This, after the environment registered with less than 1 percent of the voters as an issue of concern! To cite an example of why this nutjob believed the environment was such a hot topic for the Democrats to latch on to, he said, "I believe global warming is more important than we thought. Because I've lived through two recent hurricanes in Florida, I've come to understand the dangers of global warming."

I COULD NOT BELIEVE THIS MAN SUGGESTED A CONNECTION BETWEEN THE HURRICANES IN FLORIDA AND SUVS!

I had to put down my remote control because I was laughing so hard. I could not believe this man suggested a connection between the hurricanes in Florida and SUVs! Tell me liberalism isn't a mental disorder. In a strange way, this gives me great hope that conservative ideals will, more and more, continue to influence the shaping of America's future. Liberals seem intent on losing it.

THE ENEMY WITHIN

Not only were the Dems out of touch during the last election cycle, but they continued to miss the heart and soul of the American people. What they called *social issues* were, in fact, *socialist issues.* Which is why in each chapter I elucidate the insanities and inanities of liberalism. After all, exposing and diagnosing their mental disorder is the first step on the road to recovery.

For instance, the single biggest threat facing America is the rise of Islamofascism in this country. While the throat-cutters in dirty nightshirts beheaded Americans, the clipped hair czarinas of lower learning at a California middle school required students to pretend they were Muslims—including chanting and praying to Allah!

These clueless educators (who deny Jews and Christians the same right to pray in school) encouraged *toleraaance* for Muslims precisely at the same time many imams from the "religion of peace" were assailing American infidels. Insanity! And, at many of our colleges—which are often nothing more than houses of porn and scorn—pro-terrorist professors like Ward Churchill at the University of Colorado at Boulder spew speeches that transcend the treasonous.

> WHILE THE THROAT-CUTTERS IN DIRTY NIGHTSHIRTS BEHEADED AMERICANS, THE CLIPPED HAIR CZARINAS OF LOWER LEARNING AT A CALIFORNIA MIDDLE SCHOOL REQUIRED STUDENTS TO PRETEND THEY WERE MUSLIMS.

Fox example, ensconced in his twisted Lilliputian world, Churchill told Fox News that "Bush, at least in symbolic terms, is the world's leading terrorist. He absolutely thumbs his nose at the rule of law. He's the head of a rogue state by definition." Churchill's psychotic screed is consistent with a paper he wrote shortly after the 9/11 terrorist attack in which he compared the dead Americans to Nazi sympathizers while praising the al-Qaida suicide terrorists as "combat teams" who he celebrated as having made "gallant sacrifices" for their cause.

In case there was any dispute over his anti-American position, he told *Satya* magazine in April 2004: "I want the . . . U.S. off the planet. Out of existence altogether." Clearly, such maniacal ranting can only be explained as a byproduct of the mental disorder of liberalism.

If only we could learn a lesson from the brutal slaying of Dutch filmmaker Theo van Gogh. The Dutch are now demanding the expulsion of any imams who have not studied Islam in Holland, the closing down of any mosques that do not support Dutch values, and other sensible measures for any society wishing to survive. How I pray that this common-sense approach be enacted in America before some of our journalists end up with knives in their hearts with Arabic notes of jihad pinned to their chests.

As you'll see in Chapter Six, the bitter fruit of liberalism has produced a bumper crop of homegrown traitors. While Islamofascists stab us in the throat, the American unCivil Liberties Union (ACLU), the National Lawyers Guild, and other radical leftist organizations are stabbing us in the back. They have become a government unto themselves. No longer a shadow government because of their empowerment by vast infusions of suspicious wealth, they openly challenge our elected government, compromise our national security, and strip America of her rock-bed Judeo-Christian identity.

Anthony Romero, the pockmarked Dr. Strangelove that heads the ACLU (who, incidentally, is an openly gay man), made it clear when he took over the reins of the ACLU that he'd make gay rights the number one issue in America. Part of their agenda, then, is to strip Lady Liberty of any public display of faith. Through aggressive, rabid-dog legal terror tactics, the ACLU has carved out a cottage industry by suing communities over historical displays of the Ten Commandments and other founding documents where Judeo-Christian language is found. Apparently, Romero believes in eliminating God and the Bible to see the radical gay agenda realized.

> ANY NATION WHO REFUSES TO CONTROL HER BORDERS IS NOT JUST SUFFERING FROM A MENTAL DISORDER, THEY'RE TIPTOEING AT THE LEDGE OF A SKYSCRAPER.

Further jack hammering the foundations of our national identity and our sovereignty has been the invasion of illegal aliens. In Chapter Three, you'll see how both parties have sold us out. Every day we receive reports of Middle Eastern men shaving off their beards and disguising themselves as Mexicans who then creep over the southern border. And nothing is done to stop this human invasion.

Neither party will stop it. Worse, our president appears to be listening to his liberal advisors; Bush continues to push to grant legal-worker status to illegal aliens. No wonder that *every day* in 2004 more than 8,000 illegal aliens crossed from Mexico to America unstopped. *Every day!* Any nation who refuses to control her borders is not just suffering from a mental disorder, they're tip-toeing at the ledge of a skyscraper.

THE GOD GAP

The ultra-intolerant "liberals" of today can be recognized by several facets of character, appearance, and use of language. In the streets they generally resort

INTRODUCTION

> HERE'S A WOMAN
> [MADONNA] WHO MADE
> A CAREER AS A PSEUDO-
> PORNOGRAPHIC BELLY
> DANCER CAVORTING
> WITH A WHIP, AND NOW
> SUDDENLY AFTER
> HAVING A BABY SHE
> PRETENDS TO BE A
> HOLY WOMAN.

to petty violence and grandiloquent gestures, the agitprop of failed regimes. In speeches, they never refer to "God" but always speak of "the gods" or the "spirit force" or of a "personal god."

Thanks to the godless worldview of liberalism, America has become less oriented around faith and more a society of pagans and paganism, where the popular symbols are dream catchers and crystals hanging from rearview mirrors—all in one generation.

Or, take Madonna and the Kabala.

What does she know about Kabala? Here's a woman who made a career as a pseudo-pornographic belly dancer cavorting with a whip, and now suddenly after having a baby she pretends to be a holy woman riding her bicycle in England on her country estate with her imbecilic buddy Gwyneth Paltrow. They both fled America because America wasn't clean enough for their offspring. In Madonna's view, we're a spiritually bankrupt nation—which she helped create!

Now she's peddling Kabala water.

What could Madonna know about a sacred arm of Judaism?

Answer: Nothing.

Everybody understands that in order to even begin to understand Kabala you first have to be an expert in the Torah, which are the first five books of Moses. She skipped the five books of Moses and went right to the Kabala. For her to sell Kabala water is the equivalent of selling the fumes instead of the drink. You might say she's trying to bottle the scent of freshly brewed coffee without bothering to gather the beans, roast the beans, boil the water, and make the coffee. I suppose in the instant age of the computer and the microwave, maybe that's all the Western mind is capable of—the whiff of fresh-brewed coffee, or of holy water.

You see, thanks to the disorder of liberalism, too much that's being done in the name of faith or religion functions on a superficial level. Madonna is an example of the weakening of our spirituality.

Has a Jewish leader emerged to teach Judaism and the roots of it, the Bible? No. So, instead of having a leader who can arise to teach us about the Rock of Ages, the Bible, we have a charlatan that arises and peddles the *scent* of the Rock of Ages, and calls it the fundament itself.

Likewise, in the media and in popular language we've gone from a scientific orientation to a tribal orientation—that is, a nonscientific, primitive orientation. As we have been devolving along these lines America has been weakened. We are no longer strengthened by our knowledge. The wisdom of the West has now been reduced to an emphasis on feelings and emotions rather than reasoned thinking.

Whether speaking about faith, the plight of the poor, the needs of the elderly, or other challenges facing this nation, liberals often speak with the postures and flourishes of passion. But, when analyzed for content, their words lack substance and remind us of a flaking, ornate façade of stucco (which conceals their hollowness behind which is nothing). Their lengthy speeches are poor substitutes for a single useful idea.

Yes, the liberal may wish for justice and virtue, but my hope is that enough Americans will reject their naïve idealism before they bring total ruin upon America and themselves. Admire their ideals, but do so with reservation. Recognize their useless brilliance, their unavailing commitment, and their uncompromising convictions, but do not permit your emotions to be swayed by their call. Their ideas are foolish no matter how often and consistently they are repeated.

INTRODUCTION

It may be hard for you to comprehend that there is a significant number of fellow Americans who continue to believe that our society is doomed and not worthy of survival; that each of her institutions is unworthy of preserving and requires extermination. You see, the "progressives" may not realize they are fighting for an empty cause. Led by fools and scoundrels, they assume our nation is led by fools and scoundrels and that the U.S. is as bad or worse than the extremist Islamic state.

How this imbalance can occur in otherwise well-educated and intelligent people can only be understood through psychoanalysis. And only by the process of psychoanalysis can one reach the reasonable conclusion that such extremism in thinking is in fact a mental disorder. As more clear-thinking Americans embrace the Savage Truth about this disorder, we may yet see the complete demise of the progressives in America, their failed ideals finally consigned to history's dustbin.

In the meantime, you'll find these pages to be an oasis of sanity in a world gone mad. Here, I strip away the veneer of deceit to bring you the naked reality of the liberal body politic. It isn't always pretty, but the Savage Truth is the only antidote for the mental disorder of liberalism.

ONE

MORE PATTON, LESS PATENT LEATHER

Lock your doors—or at least find a secluded spot where you can be alone without fear of interruption. What I'm about to say may send shockwaves through your conservative sensibilities. You will either feel a jolt of clarity provoked by my Savage Truth, or you will be scandalized. That is the risk I must take. Ready?

On January 30, 2005, Iraq held their first free election in fifty years. Without question this is a great victory for democracy. More than 70 percent of eligible Iraqi voters—95 percent in several Baghdad neighborhoods—yes, Iraqis by the millions, braved suicide bombings and threats of mayhem to register their vote for freedom. While it is yet to be seen whether the ancient divisions can be forgotten, the Iraqi people are celebrating freedom today because of the sacrifice and the determination of our men and the coalition forces.

Having said that—and here's the difficult part—*I believe the Iraq War will be recorded as one of the greatest of military miscalculations.*

Before you dismiss me as a flag-burning pacifist, let me be clear: Team Bush won Operation Iraqi Freedom in a most spectacular fashion. Using sophisticated, high-tech weapons, our courageous warriors proved once again that they are the brightest and the best soldiers on the planet. Period. Their enormous superiority on the battlefield was unmatched—a lesson not missed by the world community.

Take Russia. Our previous Cold War adversary was scrutinizing our every move. Former deputy defense minister of Russia, Vitaly Shlykov, observed, "The Iraqi Army was a replica of the Russian Army, and its defeat was not predicted by our generals."[1] Vladimir Dvorkin, who heads the Russian Defense Ministry's strategic nuclear think tank, was equally stunned by our military might. He confessed, "The gap between our capabilities and those of the Americans has been revealed, and it is vast."[2]

So, why do I insist the historians and the cadets at West Point will look back on the war in Iraq as a gigantic miscalculation? Bush won the initial conflict in a brilliant display of strength. However, he struggled to maintain the peace in Iraq because he didn't have an overall strategic plan to eliminate the pockets of resistance and establish immediate control of the streets. Fighting a politically acceptable pacification does not work.

In January 2005, Iraq's new intelligence chief, Maj. Gen. Mohammed Abdullah al-Shahwani, said as much. By his estimates there are "between 20,000 and 30,000 armed men operating all over Iraq, mainly in the Sunni areas where they receive moral support from about 200,000 people."[3] These are terrorists skilled in warfare and include former members of the Ba'ath Party, army holdouts, and Islamic extremists with a death wish.

Remember how quickly Saddam's "mighty" Republican Guard threw down their arms and evaporated? Where did they disappear to? They withdrew like termites into the woodwork of the general population. While I'm not a military tactician, it's clear they wanted to sucker the Americans into thinking the battle was over. In truth, we still had to fight the real war, a guerrilla war—something our nation does not have the stomach for, not after Vietnam. We won the ground war, but they've been winning the psychological war—at least so far. That's number one.

Second, liberalism has so warped the *sensibiiilities* of Mr. and Mrs. America, Bush got trapped trying to fight a politically correct war while America's Marxist media militia, armed with zoom lenses, waited to pounce on any PC violation. As I wrote in my bestseller *The Enemy Within,* Bush's Operation Iraqi Freedom was actually fought on two fronts: He had to fight the war overseas as well as the media's war on the war effort at home.

That said, here's a prime example of their trickle-down PC stupidity. As the coalition troops were preparing for battle, one lieutenant colonel who shall remain nameless advised those under his command: "Iraq is steeped in history. It is the site of the Garden of Eden, of the Great Flood, and the birthplace of Abraham. Tread lightly there."[4]

How exactly does an Abrams tank tread lightly?

HOW EXACTLY DOES AN ABRAMS TANK TREAD LIGHTLY?

Is this a police action or a war? His view sounds like what we heard during the election of 2004 from Demoncat presidential candidate John Kerry. Kerry picked the UNITY 2004 Conference to proclaim, "I believe I can fight a more effective . . . more sensitive war."

What does that mean? Rubber bullets? Padded handcuffs and chaise lounges for POWs?

Such PC-think only gets our men killed.

Ironically, the very war John Kerry had promised is the exact war George Bush is fighting. So, rather than firebomb the Iraqi holdouts back to the Stone Age, Bush sent our boys into the rat's nest of Fallujah on a door-to-door basis as if they were selling Avon. You cannot fight a politically correct war and expect to win it. Nor can you fight a politically correct *occupation* and win it.

The fact of the matter is there was only one solution to Bush's problem—it was the same solution that's been used in warfare since the beginning of time: Total domination of the enemy, one that obliterates, neutralizes, and demoralizes the opposition.

For General George S. Patton, arguably the greatest military commander of our day, this was Job One. Patton would have used air power to flatten Fallujah—the headquarters of operations for terrorist Abu Musab al-Zarqawi—and pulverized probably the entire Sunni Triangle while he was at it. Then and only then would he have sent in the infantry for the door-to-door "clean up."

PUMMEL OR PLACATE

I understand that you might not know the difference between Patton and mutton primarily because today's history textbooks don't tell you about Ol' Blood 'n Guts Patton. About all the clipped-hair, mean-faced czarinas of education teach is how to knit flags of the United Nations and play patty-cake with your enemy.

Never a person to mince words, Patton understood the principle of domination. As he told his troops, with a cigar clamped between his teeth, "There is only one tactical principle which is not subject to change. It is to use the means at hand to inflict the maximum amount of wound, death, and destruction on the enemy in the minimum amount of time."[5]

Does that sound harsh?

It is, and it should be.

War is hell, not a video game.

When I hear our generals or the CIA or the FBI speak about the war on terrorism I have to wonder: Why do they speak in such soft, vanilla terms? Where is the fury? Frankly, we need more generals who, like Patton, recognize that "No bastard ever won a war by dying for his country. He won it by making the other poor dumb bastard die for his country."

> **"NO BASTARD EVER WON A WAR BY DYING FOR HIS COUNTRY. HE WON IT BY MAKING THE OTHER POOR DUMB BASTARD DIE FOR HIS COUNTRY."**
> **—PATTON**

Just once I'd like to see Donald Rumsfeld fire off a line like that one. Instead, Rummy made the rounds on the various talk shows talking up the war effort and how great everything was going in Iraq. He smiled for the sheeple and assured us that the provinces were subdued and the people would be voting. The next day flames flared all over the country as the suicide bombers hit the police stations, the oil installations, and U.S. military convoys.

Thirty were killed one day, forty killed another day.

Our leaders are living in a sheltered dream world, like ancient kings and queens, happily living with their cloistered delusions of success in Iraq. They continue to put out happy, cheerful news about how good everything is going while each day scores of innocent civilians are murdered by radical Islamists. Instead of taking the approach that needs to be taken, namely, a devastating air campaign against the pockets of hate, they continue to send our boys in as walking targets.

The whole Sunni Triangle should have been cleared out with leaflets in the native tongue giving civilians three days to flee to safety, and then bombed. That's what we did in World War II. What the hell is the difference between leveling cities in Germany back then and our need to demolish the terrorist hotbeds in Iraq today? Nothing. Either you're at war or you're not at war.

So why, then, are we fighting in hand-to-hand combat? For political reasons, that's why. There's no reason for our boys to be doing that, not with today's military options including the precision laser-guided bombs, the unmanned drones, and the technology that allows us to see a guy pass gas from 20,000 feet overhead.

And so our troops are stuck in a no-win situation. Not for lack of technology. Not for lack of valor. Not for lack of training or leadership in the field. But for a lack of spine from the politicians in Washington who, seeking to placate Petter Jennings and Katy "Koran" Couric of *our* Jazeera TV, refuse to allow our military to do what must be done in Iraq. Instead, the troops and the military budget remain stretched to the breaking point. Current estimates place the cost of our Iraqi presence at a breathtaking $4.5 billion *per month*.[6]

The president must take off his red baseball jacket and put on his flight jacket. We don't need a shortstop; we need a commander in chief. Unless he uses his bully pulpit to silence the media yappers while giving the order to hammer the holdouts, our boys will remain sitting ducks. Which goes back to my original view that this war has become a political military miscalculation.

What the frat boys in Washington apparently haven't learned from their pie charts and the latest PowerPoint presentation is that you must crack down on the enemy with an iron fist. We needed a swift and severe "Patton action" to squash the "insurgents" (lib-speak for terrorist scum). We got a bush-league response instead.

You're dealing with a primitive people here who lived in terror for thirty years and who understand only one thing: brute force. Actually, if you were to trace their history, you'd find that they've lived in a nightmare state for more than a thousand years, ever since the Mongols destroyed the water system that supplied Mesopotamia. Which is why they fear and respect only muscular force.

If Patton were leading our troops today, he'd probably tell the president you can't fight a guerrilla war with Mr. Rogers in a helmet. Nor can you enter a war zone acting benevolent. If you do, you leave in a six-foot pine box. At the end of the major conflict in Iraq, Bush should not have been worried about bad press; he should have immediately sent in the Bees—the B1, B2, B17, and B52 bombers—and flattened the filthy rats in dirty nightshirts in the Sunni Triangle, putting the fear of Allah in anyone who dared to resist. It's the same thing he should have done in Afghanistan—maybe then, instead of looking for a lease on a new cave, Osama would be in U.S. custody already. *Or dead.* I don't want to be choosy—I'd settle for that one too.

> IT'S THE SAME THING HE SHOULD HAVE DONE IN AFGHANISTAN—MAYBE THEN, INSTEAD OF LOOKING FOR A LEASE ON A NEW CAVE, OSAMA WOULD BE IN U.S. CUSTODY ALREADY.

Then and only then can benevolence and democracy take root.

You see, before a country can be occupied, it must be neutralized. That was true both in Germany and in Japan. It's true today in Iraq. History teaches us we couldn't have occupied Japan until their army had been defeated *and* two bombs had been dropped breaking the will of the people to fight. That's how you gain the psychological advantage over your enemy. As Sun Tzu wrote in *The Art of War,* "Kill one, terrify a thousand."

That has yet to happen in Iraq because we haven't razed any major area of the country; we're far too concerned about chipping a flake of paint off of the dome of a Mosque than crushing the terrorist crustaceans cowering inside. Nor did we round up the Iraqi military leadership and toss them into POW camps. Instead, we let them go, which is why they melted into the general population.

Imagine what would have happened in World War II if Patton had rolled into town, captured the enemy, and then sent them home with their weapons the way we did in Iraq? We would have been fighting a guerrilla war in Germany for twenty years, that's what!

Thank God Patton gave his men clear marching orders to pummel and not placate the enemy. He barked, "The Nazis are the enemy. Wade into them. Spill their blood. Shoot them in the belly. When you put your hand into a bunch of goo that a moment before was your best friend's face, you'll know what to do." In the end, 400,000 Russians had to die in Berlin before Nazism was defeated.

> **"THE NAZIS ARE THE ENEMY. WADE INTO THEM. SPILL THEIR BLOOD. SHOOT THEM IN THE BELLY. WHEN YOU PUT YOUR HAND INTO A BUNCH OF GOO THAT A MOMENT BEFORE WAS YOUR BEST FRIEND'S FACE, YOU'LL KNOW WHAT TO DO."**
> **—PATTON**

Does that sound scandalous to your modern ears?

Have you forgotten the Nazis gassed six million Jews? That Saddam killed over one million Iraqis?

You see, the mental disorder of liberalism has hoodwinked Americans into embracing the fairyland view of resolving conflict articulated by singer Sheryl Crow: "I think war is never the answer to solving any problems. The best way to solve problems is to not have enemies." Somebody should call Condi Rice with that hot tip. Crow is wrong. There are times when war is the only road to peace.

WEREWOLF: FIGHTING TOOTH AND CLAW

Even with Patton's aggressive action it took the better part of two years to ferret out the pockets of resistance. Why? In the fall of 1944 the Germans amassed a "death squad" called Werwolfs (which means "military wolf" and are also referred to as Werewolves). An estimated 6,000 diehard Nazis, Hitler youth, elite SS troops, and members of the Gestapo were specially trained to conduct guerilla attacks against the Allied Forces as well as assassinating Germans who were caught cooperating with the U.S. military.

This notorious fighting unit was taught to engage in ambushes, sniping attacks, sabotage, the roadside bombing of cars and trains, and arson. They were credited with a number of high-profile attacks including the assassinations of Dr. Franz Oppenhoff, mayor of Aachen and an outspoken anti-Nazi, Field Marshal Major John Poston, and General Berzarin, the Soviet commandant of Berlin, while also battling Soviet troops and bombing U.S. military barracks.

There is some disagreement as to the effectiveness and scope of this Nazi guerilla organization. Some have argued that the "Werwolf amounted to next to nothing" and that the "Werwolf itself was filled not so much by fearsome SS officers but teenagers too young for the front."[7] Others recognized their role in successful attacks against allied forces, but assert that "Werwolf was far weaker than many other historically significant guerrilla insurgencies, e.g. those in Vietnam and Iraq."[8]

Whatever their strengths, the similarity between the guerrilla war stratagem of the Nazis and the ongoing insurgent struggle in Iraq is difficult to ignore, a fact I pointed out on my radio show. It was likewise highlighted in several speeches before the Veterans of Foreign Wars in San Antonio, Texas, by then National Security Adviser Condoleezza Rice and by the Secretary of Defense Donald Rumsfeld. Rumsfeld said:

One group of those dead-enders was known as "werewolves." They and other Nazi regime remnants targeted Allied soldiers, and they targeted Germans who cooperated with the Allied forces. Mayors were assassinated including the American-appointed mayor of Aachen, the first major German city to be liberated. Children as young as ten were used as snipers, radio broadcasts, and leaflets warned Germans not to collaborate with the Allies. They plotted sabotage of factories, power plants, rail lines. They blew up police stations and government buildings, and they destroyed stocks of art and antiques that were stored by the Berlin Museum. Does this sound familiar?[9]

The problem with the Rummy-Rice Werwolf discussion was that they only told half of the story. Yes, the comparison with the guerilla insurgency in Iraq is a good one. However, the rest of the story was left out. What did Patton's army do when they caught a Nazi Werwolf? They shot him, that's what. The Werwolfs were tied to a lamppost and shot in the field. Our boys didn't bring them back to America to lecture at the Kennedy school of government.

> **WHAT DID PATTON'S ARMY DO WHEN THEY CAUGHT A NAZI WERWOLF? THEY SHOT HIM, THAT'S WHAT.**

But then again, there were no Ted Kennedys or Chuck Schumers holding congressional hearings to bray about the Geneva Convention. It was total war and Americans wanted it over. No, Patton had them tied to a post and shot their brains out with a seven-man firing squad. I believe that we are very near the same national attitude today, and that special El Salvador-style death squads would be approved by the American people if put to a vote.

Not only do we need special squads of guerilla hunters comprised of our best special forces, but we also need to create large internment camps in Iraq. Former members of the Ba'ath Party must be rounded up and interned until Iraq is stabilized. At that point a decision could be made how to deal with them. Perhaps war crimes trials would be in order and the most diehard Saddam loyalists executed to avoid a destabilization of the foundling nation. As Patton knew, deportation would be out of the question; these murderers would become worldwide terrorists forever.

Imagine the outcry from the neo-socialist left in our country if American troops used Patton's technique today. We got a minor taste of their anger when Lt. Gen. James Mattis spoke at a conference in San Diego and admitted it's "quite fun" to fight Iraqis and Afghans. "It's a hell of a hoot," said Mattis, "I'll be right up front with you, I like brawling."

Some in the top brass supported Mattis but "counseled" him about his rough words. The Council on American-Islamic Relations called on the Pentagon to punish this American hero. It's some of these same America-hating internal enemies who thought putting panties on the heads of prisoners at Abu Ghraib was tantamount to torture. We heard more moral outrage from the Marxist-left when U.S. soldiers placed Fruit of the Loom underwear on the heads of captured combatants than when the Hitlers in headscarves beheaded our civilians. In a time of war, liberalism is either treason or a mental disorder.

How can they forget the face of the enemy?

How can they forget radical Islam wants them dead?

How can they continue to blast our military and, in turn, weaken America's future? And why do they view this president as a greater threat to America's future than bin Laden? Don't these anarchists of the soul understand we are at a crossroads, a defining moment in the history of our Republic? We're facing a threat unlike anything we've faced before. Our soldiers defeated the communists, the fascists, and the Nazis. And now, as our military engages Islamic fanatics and their plastic martyrs, the insane media elite are bent on demoralizing our troops on the ground and the public back home.

Don't they care about their own survival?

The liberal media machine—who doesn't have the will to squash a cockroach let alone these vermin—seems to relish cutting our boys off at the knees. You see, the media, which is already more prone to report our failures than our successes, has wanted another Vietnam almost from the end of the last Vietnam. Self-loathing seems to be a permanent disfigurement from the disease of modern liberalism, and that is particularly true in foreign policy where the military is concerned.

Take Afghanistan who, thanks to its liberation from the Taliban, had its first election in which ten million voted—43 percent of whom were women. Does the media elite write stories commending our efforts that led to this historic breakthrough? No. Instead, when the media didn't get their Vietnam in Afghanistan, they turned to Iraq.

And Bush seems to be handing it to them.

Am I proposing that we leave? No. While we should have initially launched a massive air strike that razed Fallujah, we now must finish what we've started as quickly as we can—including working to stabilize the newly elected government. If we demonstrate a lack of resolve now, I predict we will pave the way for a long-term loss of millions of American lives. How? To cut and run from Iraq before the job is done—as the socialist internationalists on the left would have us do—is to embolden the enemy. They will see us as weak and, in turn, will once again bring the fight to our shores in a spectacular fashion.

I stand by those words.

HOLE IN THE COLE: HOW LIBERALS WAGE WAR

There's an invaluable lesson about the disorder of liberalism to be learned from the bombing of the *USS Cole*. This $1 billion Aegis-class guided missile destroyer is a marvel of American engineering. It was one of the premiere destroyers in our fleet with more than seventy tons of armor and equipped with unmatched radar and weaponry.

A lot of good that did on October 12, 2000. The suicidal fanatics in dirty wetsuits who almost sank the *Cole* did so with a rubber boat they probably bought at a flea market—that, and a few hundred pounds of C-4 explosives. Their makeshift torpedo ripped a $222 million, forty-by-forty foot hole in the *Cole,* killing seventeen U.S. sailors and maiming thirty-nine others.

> THE SUICIDAL FANATICS IN DIRTY WETSUITS WHO ALMOST SANK THE COLE DID SO WITH A RUBBER BOAT THEY PROBABLY BOUGHT AT A FLEA MARKET—THAT, AND A FEW HUNDRED POUNDS OF C-4 EXPLOSIVES.

Why was their dinghy allowed to approach the *Cole* when the ship was operating under "Threat Condition Bravo"—the second highest of four security warnings? Why were the sentries on the deck required to bear unloaded weapons? Why did the destroyer's rules of engagement require permission from the *Cole's* captain or another officer before firing?

I'll tell you why: Admiral Vern Clark, chief of naval operations for the Navy under Bill Clinton, said you can't have weapons that fire. The Pentagon-approved rules of engagement for the destroyer basically said you mustn't show any *hostiiility,* especially not to our Arab brethren. Even though they approached the ship from Yemen, a known terrorist strong-hold, you just never know about their true intentions. Maybe they were coming with pita bread, or to sell handmade baskets, or maybe they were just tourists wanting to take pictures with the crew as souvenirs.

The insanity of liberalism gets worse. Just look at the new marching orders: Always let the enemy take the first shot. Hard to believe?

With saltwater gushing into the bowels of the *Cole,* Petty Officer John Washak immediately trained his M-60 machine gun on a second craft that approached the *Cole's* fantail to defend the ship from another surprise attack. Unbelievably, a senior chief petty officer waved him off and told him to stand down! Even "With blood still on my face," Washak said, he was informed: "That's the rules of engagement—no shooting unless we're shot at."[10]

What? I thought they were just bombed.

The irony wasn't missed by Petty Officer Jennifer Kudrick, a sonar technician aboard the *Cole.* She said, "We would have gotten in more trouble for shooting two foreigners than losing seventeen American sailors."[11] That's what you get when you allow America-haters to transform the once great Navy into a glorified Peace Corps.

Wake up, sheeple! America has been infected by a mental disorder that is virtually destroying everything your ancestors handed to you on a silver platter. If you continue to let the neo-socialist liars from hell tie the hands of our military with their insane political correctness, then don't be surprised when the Islamofascists hit us again.

IDEALS ARE FINE: REALITY IS BETTER

There's another dimension to my assertion that President Bush appears to be mired in a military miscalculation. As a student of history, it's painfully clear to me that Mr. Bush has made essentially the same critical mistake that Jimmy Carter made in Iran. Without getting too technical, let me explain.

Carter was concerned about the human rights abuses under the shah of Iran and his secret police, the Savak. The Savak, like Saddam, tortured dissenters in a most brutal fashion. Knowing this, Carter undermined the shah's regime. The human rights abuses under the shah were real enough and needed to be addressed. I don't take issue with that fact.

However, the shah was a Western-educated, modern man who was very much an ally of the United States. By unseating the shah in order to usher in a more democratic nation, Carter inadvertently brought to power Ayatollah Khomeini who, in turn, formed the first modern Islamic republic. You may wonder what's the big deal with that. If your attention span were longer than a beer commercial, you'd know that Carter's decision means the world is suffering today as radical Islam sweeps across the globe from the epicenter of Iran!

> **IF YOUR ATTENTION SPAN WERE LONGER THAN A BEER COMMERCIAL, YOU'D KNOW THAT CARTER'S DECISION MEANS THE WORLD IS SUFFERING TODAY AS RADICAL ISLAM SWEEPS ACROSS THE GLOBE FROM THE EPICENTER OF IRAN!**

In hindsight, Carter's bleeding heart led to millions of bleeding hearts—literally.

An analogy could be made to George Bush and Iraq. If you accept that the whole reason for going to war against Saddam Hussein was because of Hussein's human rights abuses, the torture chambers, and his oppression and murder of his own people, then the analogy holds.

What has the result been?

As you'll see in a moment, by toppling the butcher of Baghdad, more instability and more radical Islamic influence has emerged, not less. Which is why we must consider whether or not President Bush has made the same mistake as Carter as a result of his humanitarian instincts. In other words, you might argue that history is repeating itself because of liberal advisors to the throne of power.

Of course, reasons other than human rights violations initially led the United States to engage in Operation Iraqi Freedom. Iraq's giving comfort, training, and aid to terrorists, as well as the potential of biological weapons, were at the top of Bush's list. No doubt oil was an issue, too. Nevertheless, the face of this war is still being sold as a humanitarian war to free the Iraqi people from an evil dictator.

That said, as we went to war there appears to have been an assumption made by the Bush administration which I'll call the "Positive Domino Effect." The Bushies believe that by giving Saddam and his Ba'ath Party the boot and by establishing a beachhead for democracy in the region, the "New Iraq" will become a beacon for freedom in the Middle East—that's the first domino.

The people of Syria and Iran and others will look to the shining city on the hill that is Baghdad with envy; they will throw off their shackles, knock over the statues, and pull down their oppressors so they, too, can have a Wal-Mart Supercenter on every corner. Just like in dominoes, tip one over and all of the dictators will fall, or so goes the theory.

The president said as much in a speech to the press on December 20, 2004. He claimed that the enemies of freedom "know that a democratic Iraq will be a decisive blow to their ambitions, because free people will never choose to live in tyranny." What Bush said is mostly true; people don't vote for tyranny. But then, would-be tyrants don't necessarily run for democratic office.

Not to be cynical, it's a bit of a stretch to think that the dictators of Syria and Iran will willingly pound their swords into plowshares. Again, what has the result of our war effort been? While it's far too early to tell whether or not Bush's Positive Domino Effect strategy will work, there is a deeper, almost haunting reality just around the corner.

SUPERSIZING IRAN

The Iraqi Shiites—whose allegiances are closer to Iran, the center of the Shi'a Islamic sect—are real happy now because we've defeated the Sunnis under Sadaam Hussein who had controlled Iraq. With this war, we've suddenly tilted the balance of power toward the Shiites. We've handed them a victory that they were unable to achieve on their own. Naturally, the Shiites are acting all smiley and as if they're our big friends, right?

Do you think they will suddenly forget their religion? Do you think they will forget the Sunni oppression? Do you think they've forgotten that we didn't get rid of Saddam back in 1992? The minute the Shiites win control, I fear they'll kick us out and rule with an iron heel.

The reason there are uprisings in the Sunni Triangle is because the old Saddam-ites of the Ba'ath Party are watching their power vanish right before their headscarves. As Ba'athists, they were the old power structure because Saddam was a Sunni—a minority people who suppressed the Shiites. Now with Saddam in prison eating out of a soup can, the Shiites await their day in the seat of power.

So what's the end game?

Here's where the military miscalculation factors into the picture. Mr. Bush and his band of neocons have had this ambitious fantasy of transforming Iraq into America-lite. However, visions of a democracy in Baghdad may be shortsighted. The Iraqi Shiites are the majority in parliament (representing 60 percent of the population), and they want an Islamic republic.

So, it may be that Bush's war will have inadvertently created a "Super Iran." How? Operation Iraqi Freedom is, in effect, creating a Shiite nation—Iraq—next door to another Shiite nation—Iran—who happens to be a founding member of the Axis of Evil.

Shiite, *schmee-ite* you say?

What's this got to do with you? Plenty.

There is the possibility that a Shiite Iraq will ally itself with Iran, a nation ruled by Shiite ayatollahs, and unify against us. Which means that the hornet's nest of radical Islam may actually *increase* in size rather than, as Bush had hoped, shrink. In sheeple terms, that means we might have just super-sized our terrorists' base.

Does that fear seem fanciful?

I'm not the only one who's saying this.

Mustafa Alani, the director of national security at the Gulf Research Center, a think-tank in Dubai, sees this as a definite possibility. Alani, who was born in Iraq, said, "The nightmare scenario in the region is that the election of an Iranian-influenced Shiite government in Iraq will lead to the creation of a 'Super Iran' emerging as a regional superpower. We are talking about a huge shift in the region's power balance."[12]

Oh, sure, there is some hatred between the Iraqis and the Iranians because of the vicious eight-year war (1980–1988) between the two countries over the Shatt al-Arab in the south. But that was Saddam's war, a Sunni's war, not a Shiite war.

Mouwaffaq al-Rubaie, national security advisor and a candidate for the United Iraqi Alliance, put it best when he said ominously, "Welcome to the new Iraq, this is the reality of Iraq where the majority are Shiite." Did I mention that the United Iraqi Alliance is a huge coalition that includes pro-*Iranian* Shiites?

If you think what I'm saying couldn't happen, if you believe that our newly liberated Shiite friends in Iraq would never stab

> IF YOU BELIEVE THAT OUR NEWLY LIBERATED SHIITE FRIENDS IN IRAQ WOULD NEVER STAB AMERICA IN THE BACK, THEN YOU DON'T KNOW HUMAN NATURE AS WELL AS DR. SAVAGE.

America in the back, then you don't know human nature as well as Dr. Savage. Let's be clear. We may have liberated the Shiites, but Americans are still *infidels*. So, with your indulgence, I'll share a page out of my childhood to help you get the picture.

SAM THE BUTCHER

When I was a kid growing up in the Bronx, my Aunt Bea was a lot like my mother in that she practically lived in the kitchen. There was something about that generation of women who just took pride in the way they fed their family. Sure, most of the time she served a cardio-toxic diet designed to kill off all of the men before they turned fifty. But there was almost always something wonderful in the oven. Day or night, I remember Aunt Bea's home smelled like Christmas morning.

Now, in our day freezer space was limited so Aunt Bea would buy her meat fresh from Sam the butcher. This was during a time when the same guy worked the meat counter his whole life. The butcher always knew your name when you came in. He'd order you a special cut of something, maybe a leg of lamb from Chicago or whatever. They were real customer-oriented back then.

Today, it's some kid with open sores and a nose ring working the meat counter. And every time you go in, it's a different guy. They don't know you from hamburger. Don't get me started.

I'd have to say that Sam came from a long line of butchers probably dating back to the Vikings. He was this stocky Russian, or maybe Ukrainian, man with oak stumps for arms, a bloodied white apron stretched tight across his belly, and a missing finger. From time-to-time I'd tag along with Aunt Bea for the entertainment value, you know, just to catch a glimpse of Sam wrestling a 300-pound side of beef in the back.

So, off we went to the market. Aunt Bea would study the fresh cuts of meat behind the refrigerated glass case as if picking out a new diamond ring. Sam would see us through the little window in the swinging door to the meat cutting room. He'd wipe his hands on his apron as he came out to greet us. He'd mumble something about the fresh this and that, holding up a few meat samples like a Turkish rug salesman offering a closer inspection of the goods.

Me? I'm counting the fingers to see if he still had all nine. With a nod, Aunt Bea would point to a roast and ask Sam to cut it into stew-sized pieces. He'd take the meat in the back and return a few minutes later with our selection wrapped in white butcher paper.

We'd get home and she'd toss it in the pot with the spices. I remember one day sitting down to eat and after one bite, she swore it wasn't the "good stuff" Sam had shown her from the display case. This happened a couple of times until Aunt Bea got wise to what Sam was doing. It dawned on her that he would sell her on the prime rib up front, but when he got to the back, he'd grab something on the order of dog meat imported from Korea instead. He figured she'd never know the difference.

One day, I asked, "Aunt Bea, why don't you just follow Sammy the Bull into the back to make sure you're not getting gypped?" She did. The next time we went to the market in the heat of a summer day, she put on an extra heavy coat, the scarf, and the matching ear muffs just to stay warm in the back where Sam cut up the beef. When she told Sam what she wanted to do, he didn't look too pleased. But what could he do?

He shrugged and grunted, "Just don't touch anything." I had no plans to lose a finger, so I stood there with my arms folded like a mannequin. I'm looking at the meat hooks, the slicers, and the meat cleavers fascinated by a world I never knew existed. The whole time Aunt Bea watched Sam like a New York City health inspector. This time she made sure we left with the good stuff. And when we got home and she cooked that meat, what a difference!

Here's the connection to our situation in Iraq.

The Shiites are just like Sam. They're glad to see us, they're glad to take our money, and they gladly appear to be our friends. But in the back room where we can't see them, the Shiites are figuring out a way to get one over on us. It's a classic case of bait and switch.

You shouldn't trust someone to deal honorably with you just because they smile when they speak your name.

Sam the butcher taught me that one.

Remember when Prime Minister Ayad Allawi flew to the White House to work with President Bush on this idea of building a Western-style democracy on the smoldering ruins of the post-Ba'athist Iraq? Standing shoulder to shoulder, Allawi gave Bush the photo op Bush needed in the Rose Garden. However, shortly after returning to Iraq, we got the word that America should not tamper with the direction of the new Iraqi order.

This is why I am convinced that an Islamic Republic with a strong leaning towards a modern-day theocracy will emerge in Iraq just as it did in Afghanistan. In fact it's already happening. Look at what the Iraq interim constitution has tucked between the pages of this initial governing document. It reads: *"Islam is the official religion of the State and is to be considered a source of legislation."*[13] What's this? Will the hard-line Islamic law dictate Iraqi law?

We saw the same theocratic governing formula used in Afghanistan. The unapologetic embrace of Islam in their constitution is unmistakable. It states:

Article 1—Afghanistan is an Islamic Republic, independent, unitary, and indivisible state.

Article 2—The religion of Afghanistan is the sacred religion of Islam. Followers of other religions are free to perform their religious rites within the limits of the provision of law.

Article 3—No law can be contrary to the sacred religion of Islam and the values of this Constitution.[14]

What's more, the votes from Iraq's historic election in January 2005 were being counted as my book went to press. Leading the pack with 2.2 million out of the 3.3 million counted votes was a radical Shiite cleric with direct ties to Iran—the Grand Ayatollah Ali al-Sistani—who maintained a commanding lead over the next closest contender. If Sistani is elected, I believe George Bush may have unknowingly been the handmaiden of a radical Islamic state in Iraq!

Why do I say that?

If Sistani comes to power, this newly-elected, Iranian-born leader of Iraq is sure to act in cahoots with Iran, in which case we might just see a surge of radical Islam in the region. Why? Because we don't know if Sistani will be an *ally* of Iran or an *instrument* of Iran.

Furthermore, Sistani is already on record as calling for Islam to be "recognized in law as the religion of the majority of Iraqis." And, as the favorable election results poured in, a spokesman for Sistani quickly outlined the radical position that Islam should serve as the sole basis for law and the new Iraqi constitution: "We warn officials against a separation of the state and religion, because this is completely rejected by the ulema [clergy] and marja [clerics] and we will accept no compromise on this question." In other words, while American democracy practices a separation of church and state, the emerging Islamic leadership in Iraq is demanding the rule of the church *over* the state. So, before the world gets caught up in the cheers and the "blue fingers" of Iraqi voters dipped in ink as a symbol of freedom, we might want to wait and see if an Islamic state arises. All of the blue fingers in the world won't save us if Sistani makes Islam the law of Iraq, which now appears inevitable.

I'd say George Bush's dream of an American-styled melting pot democracy serving as a beacon of freedom in the Middle East may not only be a long shot, but it demonstrates a naïve understanding of the deep-seated, often divisive ethnic and religious orientation of the Iraqi people. Its people groups are distinct, living in distinct regions, and would rather fight than blend their identities.

America as a melting pot worked here. Why? Because America was an almost empty melting pot when the Founding Fathers forged our future. Immigrants came by dribs and drabs to our shores fully expecting to jump into the collective pot—although that is now changing as the mental disorder of liberalism erases our borders, language, and culture. Try as Bush may, Iraq cannot become a melting pot as long as it insists on a national religion—especially when that religion is Islam, which, by definition, has zero tolerance for those with nonconforming views. Nor is there a good reason to expect that if we turn up the heat, the various warring factions and hostilities boiling under the surface will suddenly and happily blend together. It's bound to explode.

> IRAQ CANNOT BECOME A MELTING POT AS LONG AS IT INSISTS ON A NATIONAL RELIGION—ESPECIALLY WHEN THAT RELIGION IS ISLAM, WHICH, BY DEFINITION, HAS ZERO TOLERANCE FOR THOSE WITH NONCONFORMING VIEWS.

A good example is the former Yugoslavia, a country that didn't really work, either. It was a Cold War fiction. The various ethnic groups stuck to their regions and religions, nursed ancient hatreds for each other, and were nominally held together by the dictator Tito behind the Iron Curtain with the Soviet sledgehammer hanging over them like a Sword of Damocles. But when that tyrant's stranglehold of the people ended with his death, and when the Iron Curtain collapsed, Yugoslavia as a country fragmented.

It's time to take the blinders off. Let's stop with the hearts and flowers and the goodwill this and that. We know that the emerging government in Iraq will be an Islamic republic of some sort. We also know that a number of powerful individuals vying for leadership in the new National Assembly have direct ties to Iran.

Suddenly, we're several steps closer to the reality of a Super Iran than a U.S.-style democracy. It's fine, even admirable, that George Bush wants to advance the cause of liberty and freedom. And I'm glad that the mayor of Baghdad wants to erect a statue in Mr. Bush's honor. However, just like Jimmy Carter, who let his humanitarian feelings drive his logic, Bush has to remember that your heart is supposed to be within your chest, not between your ears. What should Bush do now?

Read on.

THE SAVAGE SOLUTION

While the longterm outcome is still in flux, the only way to both stop the constant violence in Iraq and to prevent the creation of a Super Iran may be to repartition Iraq and put it under the jurisdiction of four sovereign nations. Heresy, you say? After all, isn't Iraq a sacred nation with firm boundaries predating Moses? No.

I don't blame you for the confusion. Many of you don't know your Middle East history. The closest thing you've studied is Tolkien's Middle Earth, and that's a whole different story. What your history teacher didn't teach you is that Iraq, a creation of the British, was carved out of the old Ottoman Empire. On November 11, 1920, Iraq was formally recognized as the "State of Iraq" and remained under British control for several more years.

Why is this important?

If we are to seriously consider repartitioning Iraq as a means to

> **MANY OF YOU DON'T KNOW YOUR MIDDLE EAST HISTORY. THE CLOSEST THING YOU'VE STUDIED IS TOLKIEN'S MIDDLE EARTH, AND THAT'S A WHOLE DIFFERENT STORY.**

end the internal violence and to avoid the creation of a Super Iran, it helps to know we're not tampering with ancient biblical boundaries. There's no point bringing down God's wrath in the process. Iraq is an arbitrary creation, a fiction if you will. Modern Iraq's borders don't follow any tribal or ethnic divisions. This is especially true of its eastern border with Iran. So if it's already a fiction, why not tell a better story?

As radical as this proposal may appear, the seeds of my idea have been around a while. We heard such talk during the first Gulf War; then in 1999 reports began circulating in the Arab newspapers citing unnamed diplomatic sources that U.S. Defense Secretary William Cohen was touring the Gulf States trying to drum up support for divvying up Iraq.[15]

Here's how this repartitioning would look.

We'd take the northern region and give it to Turkey, specifically to the Turkish Kurds. Kuwait would be offered the south. The western area would be assigned to Syria as part of a peace deal where they must recognize Israel's sovereignty. And, as an olive branch to Iran, we would give them a slice of the eastern region if they agreed to dismantle their nuclear program. Then, let each of these four nations manage what is, for the most part, mountainous tribal land.

The final brush stroke in this emerging piece of art would be to paint a boundary around Baghdad at the center of the territory and call that Iraq. If we really wanted to be creative, we could give a piece to Palestine. You might get them to migrate from Gaza if there were oil wells in the deal. This would be their ticket out of the slums and into more productive land.

This creative solution to managing the New Iraq is possible because each of the countries involved would manage their portions quite differently than how we, as outsiders, are trying to handle this. I believe you wouldn't see many suicide bombings after the partition. Of course, this is only possible after a massive bombing campaign of the terrorist strongholds.

I'm not the only one exploring this idea. Ivan Eland, a senior fellow and director of the Center on Peace and Liberty at The Independent Institute in Oakland, California, made a similar suggestion on my radio program in May 2004 and in his article titled, "Thinking the Unthinkable: Partition Iraq."

I maintain it's not unthinkable at all, but pretty much the only way out of the present situation.

Likewise, Peter Galbraith, a former U.S. ambassador to Croatia and fellow at the Center for Arms Control and Non-Proliferation, pitched partition in the *New York Book Review* pages in April 2004. Galbraith knows the area well. He documented Saddam's atrocities against the Kurds for the Senate Foreign Relations Committee back in the late 1980s, and he's been advocating for the Kurds ever since.

Others, like Leslie Gelb, an assistant secretary in Jimmy Carter's State Department and then diplomatic correspondent for the *Old York Times,* and retired Army Lieutenant Colonel Ralph Peters, have been writing about this for nearly two years. The growing sentiment is that keeping the warring factions of Iraq united under one house in Baghdad cannot work. I agree.

Now, you might wonder who will administer this transition to partition. The U.S. must put together a coalition of the willing. Believe me, when there's land and oil at stake, there will be a lot of countries willing to cooperate.

My fear is that we lack someone like Patton to pull off this partition plan. We have too much patent leather. We need Patton. Bush must be at the front and center of this conflict. He got us into this quagmire. Now, I want him to stand up and tell us where he's at and where he's going. Either we'll follow him or we won't. But this nonsense of hiding and indecision has to stop. As Patton once said, "Lead me, follow me, or get out of my way."

> **AS PATTON ONCE SAID, "LEAD ME, FOLLOW ME, OR GET OUT OF MY WAY."**

I hate to say it, but we have no clear leadership from either party regarding an Iraq policy. They're all ducking and hiding and covering. They're going to the pollsters and the advisors who don't know their behinds from their elbows.

I don't know about you, but I don't want to see us leaving Iraq with our tails between our legs. I don't want to think that our men and women died for nothing. I don't want to send a signal to the rest of the world that America is weak, that we give up when the going gets difficult, that we lack the leadership to make the hard choices—be that squashing the terrorists' Iraq, standing by the newly created government, or initiating a push to repartition that troubled land.

Mark my words, what happens in Iraq directly affects what will happen at home in the future. I am not happy that Bush may have stumbled into a blunder of historic proportions. Unlike the Marxist America-haters who rejoice when our military falters, I take no pleasure in pointing out the harsh reality of our situation.

Rather, I am driven by a raw, unadulterated love for this country—the greatest nation in the history of the world. I'll be damned if I'm going to leave America a worse place than the country I inherited. You see, I'm an immigrant's son. My grandfather fled from the oppression of Europe. He came to America and worked his heart out just to bring his wife and children to the safety of our shores for a taste of freedom. He died a few years later.

Why did he work himself literally to death?

He wanted his children and grandchildren to have a better life. My immigrant dad did have a better life for a while and then he worked until his heart blew out. He, too, wanted me to enjoy the richness of this land. And I'm grateful for his sacrifices.

Now as our soldiers are fighting terrorism and, yes, for our very survival, I refuse to broadcast cheers for Team Iraq while the mental disorder of liberalism hamstrings our efforts to democratize that nation.

Nor should you.

TWO

UNMASKING ISLAMOFASCISM

John Europe hit the dirt face down, hands twisted and bound behind his back. Towering over him, a robed, hooded man barked orders in a foreign tongue. Salty droplets of sweat fell from his executioner's coarse beard, stinging John's face as his head was yanked skyward.

John caught sight of the sun as the scimitar whistled toward his pale, outstretched neck. Less than a few seconds remained before the cold, hardened steel severed John's racing heart from his head. He strained but could not remember the name of his father's God. In a flash of memory, all he could think of was a line from Charles Dickens's *A Tale of Two Cities*. As a child, John had smuggled the contraband tome from a smoldering burn pile in front of his public school.

Even now, he clung to the forbidden words: *". . . it is a far, far better rest that I go to than I have ever known."*

A sudden shriek of praises to Allah by his executioner squelched the memory. For a pitiful moment, John screamed for mercy. His agonizing appeal for grace competed with the barbaric praises of his captor, creating an unholy cacophony of sound. With the force of a lightning bolt, the blade crashed against his flesh. The hot steel found its mark. John's final wail lingered in the air as his lifeless form collapsed earthward.

His wife, Jane Europe, fought back a flood of tears as the hooded barbarian dangled John's bloodied head high above the cheering mob. And, while deeply distressed by her husband's execution at the hand of the new Islamic Purity Squad, she knew she must remain silent—or suffer the same fate. Even now the Islamists ruling her continent were trying to convince her they were not that bad. The mullahs, after all, were gracious enough to permit her to collect her husband's head and torso and to bury them in a cemetery without crosses.

* * *

Welcome to the United Islamic State of Europe, year 2075. Paranoid delusions?

Guess again—if you dare to face the Savage Truth.

You see, radical Islam isn't a religion as much as it is a political movement with global aspirations. Its leadership masquerades in holy robes, while carrying the Koran in one hand and an AK in the other. Their goal? To convert you or kill you, that's all. Nothing short of total victory will do. And, with one-fifth of the earth's population subscribing to Islam, the radical fringe is working overtime to infiltrate the rest, break our will, and drag the world back to the thirteenth century.

> RADICAL ISLAM ISN'T A RELIGION AS MUCH AS IT IS A POLITICAL MOVEMENT WITH GLOBAL ASPIRATIONS. . . . THEIR GOAL? TO CONVERT YOU OR KILL YOU.

Forget what you've been told by the "Enlightened Ones" on the left— that Islam is a religion of peace. It's all garbage. What the libs really mean is that Islam is a "religion of *pieces*" since the extremist followers of

Muhammad maim, behead, and destroy all who refuse to bend the knee to Allah. Don't take my word for it. Read the Koran for yourself.

Here's a real sapphire of a religious proverb: "I will cast terror into the hearts of those who disbelieve. Therefore strike off their heads and strike off every fingertip of them" (Koran 8:12). How do you like that one? Does the name Nicholas Berg come to mind? How about Daniel Pearl? Paul Johnson? Kim Sun-Il? Eugene Armstrong? Raja Azad? Sajjad Naeem? Decapitated, every last one of them.

These Islamic headcutters in headscarves are so warped, they consider beheadings nothing more than a Kodak moment to share with friends, followers, and foes alike. They get their video camera rolling, read some rambling message of how radical Islam should rule the world, then these insects saw off the heads of their victims with short knives. Why?

Let's let Muhammad field that one: "So when you meet in battle those who disbelieve, then smite the necks until when you have overcome them . . . and [as for] those who are slain in the way of Allah, He will by no means allow their deeds to perish" (Koran 47:4). In other words, beheadings are just part of the Islamic outreach program. They go hand-in-knife with following the will of Allah and the spread of radical Islam. Nothing more. And the liberals want us to believe this is just a religious *preeeeference.* Something we in the West should try to *understaaaand.*

Not me.

I say if Islam is such a peaceful religion, maybe they should begin by lightening up on murdering the people with whom they disagree.

Don't think for one minute this jihad is just the polite twisting of a few arms to bring infidels around to the Islamic way of living. The jihad that Muhammad called for is nothing short of world terrorism. Read the evidence for yourself: "Allah's Apostle said, '. . . I have been made victorious with terror'" (Bukhari Vol. 4, Bk. 52, No. 220); and "Allah's Apostle said, 'Killing disbelievers is a small matter to us'" (Tabari IX:69).

To these enemies of civility, it's perfectly fine to sacrifice human life if it serves the cause of making their version of Islam the dominant religion in the world. What's more, seventy-two burka-free virgins await them on the other side should they die in the service of Allah.

> **WAKE UP AND SMELL THE DIRTY BOMBS. . . . THE THROAT-SLITTERS ARE CLAWING AT THE GATE.**

Wake up and smell the dirty bombs: The march of radical Islam is the most dangerous threat to America—and the rest of the civilized world—unless they are stopped. Of course, Hillary Rodman Clinton doesn't see things as clearly as I do. In her view, "Islam is the fastest-growing religion in America, a guide and pillar of stability for many of our people."[1] The throat-slitters are clawing at the gate.

What world is she living in?

Islam is growing so rapidly within Europe that historian Bernard Lewis sees Europe becoming "part of the Arabic west." The continent will essentially be annexed by Islam. And not too far down the road, either. Lewis told the German newspaper *Die Welt* that "Europe will be Islamic by the end of the century."[2]

Of course, the Islamification of Europe could come sooner, too. Much sooner if the broken-record leftists don't stop chanting "Give peace a chance" between their yoga lessons. And don't for one second think that the Islamists will be happy just snapping the crosses off of every sacred structure in Europe.

America is next.

As the West confronts Islamic terrorism, there's one fact we forget to our mortal peril: These subhumans would just as quickly slit your throat as look at you.

I'd suggest you read that again.

I realize this harsh reality might be hard for you to comprehend, especially if you're a product of public school education where *seeensitivity* toward Muslim terrorists is taught in first period—right after the principal conducts Rahmadan prayers with a bullhorn by the United Nations flag array in the parking lot.

That doesn't change the nature of these barbarians.

What's more, their brand of hatred and intolerance is nothing new. Islamic terrorism has been around for hundreds of years, as you'll see in a minute. So let's drop all the cant and spin about how Islam is a religion of peace. I don't buy it for one second. Nor should you—that is, if you care about your survival.

TEA WITH TERRORISTS

Muslims have had a long, dark tradition of relentless violence committed against "infidels." That's a fact of history. But you don't know that, do you? You're probably one of the sheeple who spent more time in high school history class thinking about your girlfriend's cup size than the lesson. Which is not to say that your teacher would have been all that truthful about Islam's violent past *had* you been listening.

Just to be clear, an infidel is anyone who doesn't believe in Islam. Again, the goal of radical Islam is to convert you or kill you. Period. Hard to believe? Tell that to nineteen-year-old Javaid Anjum who suffered electric shocks to various body parts, a fractured arm, smashed fingers, lacerations all over his body, and—did I mention?—his nails had been pulled out.

His crime?

In April 2004, Javaid, a university student in Pakistan, was traveling to his grandfather's house when he got thirsty. He saw an outside water tap and took a drink. When confronted, he made the mistake of mentioning that he was a Christian to several Muslim *seminary* students who had accused him of stealing. The Muslims immediately dragged Javaid into their seminary where they tried to convince him through *five days of torture* to renounce his faith and embrace Islam, the religion of peace.

Evidently, Javaid didn't feel the love.

After they were done torturing Javaid, they dumped him off at the police station, charging him with theft. The police, seeing his many wounds and contusions, permitted his family to take him to the hospital. Javaid died there from two failed kidneys shortly after making a statement about the way he had been treated. Get this. No police action was taken against the Muslim torture squad! But wait, there's more. The chief constable in charge of this miscarriage of justice said it was "God's will" for Javaid to die as he did.[3]

This is not an isolated event, though I wish it were.

I'll give you another one that the media doesn't want you to know. In May 2004, Muslim youths bearing machetes and clubs slaughtered upwards of 600 Christians in Nigeria. These Islamic holy rollers burned a dozen churches, while torching houses with families trapped inside. Among the dead Christians were children. One eyewitness confirmed that "the bodies of pregnant women were ripped open and their bodies burned."[4] Within days of the rampage, some 30,000 residents of Kano, mostly Christians, were run out of town.

A massacre on that scale should be a real hot news piece. The media in this country could milk that one for days. Did CBS's Dan Forger report that?

Why am I not surprised when I hear about mobs of Muslim youth hacking scores of innocent people? If you were to dig through the earliest and most credible sources of Islamic writings, namely, the Hadiths of Ishaq, Bukhari, Tabari, and the Koran, you'd be stunned by the violent teachings and beliefs held by the "religion of peace." These Muslim youth are just practicing what their faith teaches. Can you blame them?

Kids will be kids.

Which begs the question: Why do the left and the media elite in America give radical Islam a pass? As I wrote in my bestseller, *The Enemy Within,* it's because they hope to see Islam spread in America in order to overcome the hated Christian. That's it. And, like the enemy within that they are, these pleasers and appeasers will sell America out if we let them. These quitters and quislings are pulling a dirty fleece over our eyes to keep us from knowing the true nature of our enemy.

But you probably thought your socialist sociology professor from Harvard was a genuine peacemaker when he encouraged you to reach out and *understaaaand* your terrorist brother.

I'd say he's nothing more than a peace-faker.

You want to know the truth about this foe?

Go find one of those dusty history books on religion—something printed before the politically correct revisionists took the Big Eraser to the dark chapters of this religion of peace. In the seventh century, while his neighbors were stealing each other's flocks and worshiping rocks, the prophet Muhammad supposedly took some dictation from the archangel Gabriel. The text became the Koran, and, thanks to Muhammad's cronies and heirs, the world has never been the same since its inception.

Like Christianity, Islam spread quickly. But unlike Christianity, Islam spread through violent conquest.

With swords, not sacraments.

With pillaging, not preaching.

Islam spread so quickly that, within a century of its birth, vast swathes of the known world were bowing toward Mecca five times daily: In the year 632, Jerusalem fell to the sword of Muslim armies. Alexandria in 642. Carthage in 670. Spain in 711.

Followers of Islam continued to annex whole nations and entire regions, bringing millions of people under their control. They were finally stymied by Christian "crusaders" in the Middle Ages, though it still took hundreds of years before the last major Islamic government—the Ottoman Empire—was defeated in World War I by the West. Not that tossing the Turks marked the end of Islam. Its followers are doing as much now, if not more, to spread Islam anew to regions which were in earlier times under its iron grip.

FROM SPANISH KNIGHTS TO SPANISH NIGHTS

While the Spanish knights during the glory days of Spain drove the Islamofascists out, today's inherited class of weaklings are too busy in the discotheques at night to stand up and fight for their homeland. We're seeing the same lack of resolve in America.

So why am I rehashing history?

Because we in the West are reliving it. Granted, it's a more subtle and insidious onslaught, but an onslaught nonetheless—one that might ultimately prove more lethal. Did you know that? Probably not. The problem is that you probably hate history. You don't know the difference between Genghis Khan and Chaka Khan. As the great philosopher George Santayana has said, "Those who do not know history are condemned to repeat it"!

Look, I understand nobody teaches real history in school these days. But being ignorant of history doesn't change the roots of our current crisis. The fact of the matter is that today's radical Islam leaders

> THE PROBLEM IS THAT YOU PROBABLY HATE HISTORY. YOU DON'T KNOW THE DIFFERENCE BETWEEN GHENGIS KHAN AND CHAKA KHAN.

are power-hungry vermin who advocate the subordination of all other religions and governments to their version of Islam—by any and all means, without regard to human life. They do *not* want to co-exist. They want to conquer and control.

Listen to Winston Churchill, that political statesman who exposed communism's threat to the West. In his analysis, Islam, "which above all others was founded and propagated by the sword—the tenets and principles of which are . . . incentives to slaughter and which in three continents had produced fighting breeds of men—simulates a wild and merciless fanaticism."[5]

Tell me this is a religion of peace.

LIBERALS TURN A BLIND EYE

Before the spokemouths of the left denounce this as an anti-Muslim screed, let me say that this is not a blanket condemnation of Islam or all Muslims. Far be it from me to drop the gavel on another man's faith. If you want to worship God, a cow, or a gnat for that matter, that's fine. I'll be the first to say that Islam doesn't kill people—*Islamists* do. But that's just the point. Every single major terrorist attack against the United States has been committed by radical Muslims.

> EVERY SINGLE MAJOR TERRORIST ATTACK AGAINST THE UNITED STATES HAS BEEN COMMITTED BY RADICAL MUSLIMS.

Not Christians.

Not Jews.

Not Buddhists.

Not Jehovah's Witnesses, Hindus, Mormons, New-Agers, or Jains. Am I the only guy who sees this?

Now, I realize some may point to Timothy McVeigh's Oklahoma City bombing as an example of "Christian" terrorism on American soil. They couldn't be more wrong. McVeigh wasn't a Christian, that's number one. In fact, the opposite is true. The *Atlanta Journal-Constitution* reported that McVeigh was "an avowed agnostic" his entire life up until the last hour before his execution when he requested to see a Catholic priest. This last act of a dead man walking "surprised everyone who knew him."[6]

Author Dan Herbeck had a number of conversations with McVeigh about the afterlife and concluded McVeigh clearly didn't have any convictions about faith: "He told us that when he finds out if there's an afterlife, he will improvise, adapt, and overcome, just like they taught him in the Army."[7] Christianity, on the other hand, teaches that a decision of faith must be made on this side of the grave. If McVeigh were a Christian, he would have known improvising at the gates of hell is a bad bet. Again, if McVeigh embraced Christianity, he would have known that Jesus himself taught his followers to "turn the other cheek," not blow up innocent men, women, and children.

There is absolutely no basis for the "Christian terrorist" label assigned by the media to Timothy McVeigh. Why, then, did the press (wrongly) portray McVeigh as such? Columnist Maggie Gallagher found that the label first appeared six days after the attacks of 9/11 primarily to dilute the fact that Muslim terrorists had just killed 3,000 Americans! She notes:

> On Sept. 17, 2001, a *San Francisco Chronicle* columnist blurted: "The hijackers are no more typical Muslims than Timothy McVeigh is a typical Christian." On Oct. 4, a *USA Today* columnist picked up the refrain, describing Sept. 11 terrorists as having "more in common with Timothy McVeigh, whose twisted paramilitary take on Christian retribution led him to avenge the Davidians' death."

The Christian terrorist label stuck, but the truth was not served. If anything, McVeigh's motivation for bombing the Oklahoma City federal building can be traced to anti-government rants in *The Turner Diaries* penned by William Pierce, a neo-Nazi. McVeigh was captivated by this piece of garbage. Which is why the hard-left pundit Barbara Ehrenreich knew to describe McVeigh as "America's homegrown neo-Nazi mass murderer."[8] Enough already with the patent lies and deceptions comparing McVeigh's non-faith to the acts of hate by radical Islam. It's a smokescreen to hide the truth.

And so I must ask the difficult question regarding radical Islam: What kind of religion would specialize in worldwide terror unless a viral infection of vindictiveness lurked within? All of the evidence points to the fact that such hatred must dwell within the minds of Islamists.

Some might argue that our enemy is Islam itself—not just Allah's bomb-tossing brigade, those unhappy Hitlers in headhoods. Not me. I believe it's wrong to condemn an entire faith because of a few arsenic-laced bad apples. The overwhelming majority of moderate Muslims do live peaceful lives in spite of what the prophet Muhammad taught.

The lefties can drone all day long about multiculturalism and tolerance, diversity and sensitivity. But while they trip over their apologies for jihadists, they're brain-dead to the fact that where strict Islam flourishes—especially the fundamentalist strains of the faith—the first things under the camel's cloven foot are everything they love: women's freedom, democracy, pluralism, civil rights, and liberties.[9]

General George S. Patton, writing in Casablanca in 1943, was well aware that Islam detests progress. He pondered, "What if the Arabs had been Christians? To me it seems certain that the fatalistic teachings of Muhammad and the utter degradation of women is the outstanding cause for the arrested development of the Arab. He is exactly as he was around the year 700, while we have kept on developing."[10]

More than a half-century later, it is this backward, stagnant culture that radical Muslims are trying to ram down the throats of the world. Indeed, Islamists have a bloody axe to grind with the West and its values.

You might be wondering how the surge of fundamentalist Islam matters to you. I'll tell you. Think for a moment about your cherished freedom of expression.

Think of your freedom of religion.

Think of your freedom of speech.

Think of your freedom of the written word.

Think of your freedoms, period.

> LIKE A HOT LAVA FLOW, THIS INSIDIOUS DEATH-CULTURE HAS OOZED ACROSS THE GLOBE, CONSUMING ONE CITY, ONE COMMUNITY, ONE REGION AT A TIME.

Now, release them. You see, Islam is about *submission* and *control,* not *freedom.* They fear freedom. In fact, the word "Islam" means "submission."[11] Unlike the radical belief held by our Founding Fathers that all men are endowed by their Creator with certain inalienable rights to life, liberty, and the pursuit of happiness, these throwbacks maintain the notion that women must be bound up in a burka, and their faces covered.

What ought to seize our attention is the steady pace and relentless push of Islam, radical or otherwise, around the world. Like a hot lava flow, this insidious death-culture has oozed across the globe, consuming one city, one community, one region at a time.

ONWARD, MUSLIM SOLDIERS

Muslim radicals are on the march.

From France to Spain to Denmark, Muslim centers are expanding in both political and cultural influence. In virtually *every case* the more these Islamic communities spread, the more friction is sparked with surrounding Western cultures. They have migrated throughout the European continent in the past several decades and are slowly entrenching themselves. In most stations of their sojourn, they are not yet the top dogs. But take a look at the blonde bellwether of Scandinavia to see where things are headed.

Increasingly, it's bye-bye Vikings—hello Wahhabis.

Take the city of Malmø, Sweden, for instance, which has become an outpost of the Middle East. According to the Swedish publication *Aftonbladet,* "The police now publicly admit what many Scandinavians have known for a long time: They no longer control the situation in the nation's third-largest city. It is effectively ruled by violent gangs of Muslim immigrants. . . ."

Ripping a page from America's Mexican immigration problem, some Muslims who have lived in Malmø for twenty years still can't speak or write a lick of Swedish. Worse, ambulance personnel are stoned and attacked and now refuse to enter certain areas without police protection; in turn, citizens are dying before receiving help. Sometimes even the police won't go in without heavy backup for fear they'll be attacked or their cars vandalized.[12]

As reporter Robert Spencer details, there are other alarming developments:

- The Nordgårdsskolen school in Aarhus, Denmark, has *no* Danes enrolled; every student is Muslim.

- In Denmark, the Koran is now required reading for all upper-secondary school students, a development that is alarming because (a) it demonstrates the scope of Muslim influence; and (b) any sort of single-source fundamentalist religious content should never be "required reading" or study in a public-school setting.

- Qazi Hussain Ahmed, a Pakistani Muslim leader, was allowed into Norway to give a speech in Oslo despite his earlier public praise of al-Qaida leader Osama bin Laden and his party, Jamaat-e-Islami.

- As of fall 2004, Dutch officials have discovered more than a dozen terrorist plots, each one aimed at punishing the Netherlands for contributing 1,300 troops to U.S.-led coalition forces in Iraq.

- Other nations have been held to account by Islamists for their participation in the Iraq invasion. The Philippine government, for example, agreed to withdraw its small military contingent from Iraq after Muslim terrorists kidnapped a Filipino truck driver in July 2004.

- In Spain—scene of a massive Islamist-oriented terror attack on the railways on March 11, 2004, that killed nearly 200 people, injured 2,000 more, and toppled the ruling government—Moroccan Muslims (including some suspected of taking part in the March attacks) took control of a Spanish prison in the fall of that same year, broadcasting Muslim prayers at high volume, physically intimidating non-Muslim prisoners, and hanging pictures of Osama bin Laden. "We are going to win the holy war!" they bragged, prompting the guards to ask sheepishly if the ringleaders would simply lower the volume on the prayers.[13]

Are you beginning to get the picture?

There is an undeniable imperialist and despotic streak that runs through some strains of Islam because of the doctrine of jihad. Today, with the migration of moderate Muslims to the West, we typically don't see as much friction as is evident in the blood-smattered pages of history.

Nevertheless, radicals are quick to move alongside the moderates. These infil-traitors prefer dirty bombs to diversity.

Just as troubling are their efforts to recruit from among these more moderate ranks. Yossef Bodansky, director of the Congressional Task Force on Terrorism and Unconventional Warfare, points alarmingly to the "flow of thoroughly westernized Muslims in Western Europe into the ranks of the would-be terrorists. Moreover, there is a radicalization and alienation of ever greater segments of the Muslim world even if only a relatively few resort to violence."[14]

Really? Let's say he's right about that "handful" of Muslims who resort to violence. I ask you, how many radical Muslims does it take to fly a plane into a tall building? How many does it take to plant a bomb along a train track in Spain? How many are needed to hold several hundred innocent children hostage at a school in Russia and shoot them dead in the gym?

Just a handful.

Where's the outcry from the peace-loving, moderate mullahs when fellow Muslims murder children in cold blood? Why the silence? Why no outcry? There was hardly a peep of protest coming from the mosques around the world. Have these "moderate" Muslims become at least an accessory to the crime because of their silence?

Let's take that a step further.

Remember when the Catholic Church was confronted with "a handful" of cases of sexual abuse by pedophile priests in Boston? The Righteous Ones in the media were quick to demand the head of Cardinal Bernard Law served on a platter. His crime? Neglect. He neglected to root

> **WHERE'S THE OUTCRY FROM THE PEACE-LOVING, MODERATE MULLAHS WHEN FELLOW MUSLIMS MURDER CHILDREN IN COLD BLOOD?**

out the perverts in the ranks. The guy did the right thing and stepped down to make things right. Fine.

But, there's a huge difference between *neglecting to do your job* and *slicing the throats of fellow humans*. So, let's connect the dots. When Muslim terrorists slashed and then paraded around with the heads of innocent victims, literally, the media's Righteous Ones were AWOL. The pancake-faced, leg-crossers reading their teleprompters didn't dare utter one word of outrage over these contemptible deeds.

Do you see what's going on here?

All Christians bad; only Muslim terrorists bad.

WILL THE REAL MUHAMMAD PLEASE STAND UP?

Saint or sinner? Prophet or terrorist?

The left holds up Muhammad as their little darling of faith. To the mean-faced, clipped-hair czarinas of lower learning and the Upper West Side Manhattano cocktail-types, Islam is politically *chic*. That's why you find these libs heading for the now-fashionable Muslim restaurants to dine on oxtail soup, chicken biryani, and mataba. I've seen their type. They drift in the door, bowing, hands folded together just to show how sensitive and multi-culti they are. In reality they're just impressed with their own goodness.

> ASK A MUSLIM, AND THEY'LL TELL YOU THAT MUHAMMAD WAS SINLESS. MAYBE SO. I NEVER MET THE MAN.

But what gets me is that these phonies don't have the slightest idea what the Koran teaches. They couldn't name two facts about the Muhammad they adore—or even one line from the Koran if their life depended on it.

Let's start with the basics. Ask a

Muslim, and they'll tell you that Muhammad was sinless. Maybe so. I never met the man. However, unlike Jesus, who also professed to be without sin, history demonstrates that Muhammad *loved* his women. That's an understatement. Depending on who's counting, Muhammad had between sixteen and twenty-two wives . . . not including concubines. His youngest wife, Aisha1,[15] was six years old,[16] which in every state, with the possible exception of Massachusetts, would make him a pedophile.

At twenty-five, Muhammad married his first wife, Khadijah (a woman fifteen years his senior), who just happened to be a very *wealthy* businesswoman. Upon Khadijah's death, the fidelity gig was up. He married a parade of women for a variety of reasons while drawing the line at four wives for his followers. Look, I'm no expert in these matters, but it seems to me that there's something wrong with the picture when, at fifty-four years of age, Muhammad consummated his marriage with Aisha, who was then nine.[17]

Another fact concealed by the followers of Islam is that there are actually *two* versions of the Koran: the fundamentalist, hard-core Arabic edition and the watered down, coffeehouse-blended English tea translation.[18] In other words, the paperback copy of the Koran issued to you on your first day of college is not the whole story.

See if you can guess why the rough stuff was cut out from the English version.

What amazes me is the screaming silence coming from the women's movement, especially in light of how these Islamofascists treat their females. Did you know that a man, for instance, has the right to beat his wife? Read the Koran, Surah 4:34, which, after stating that men should protect and maintain the women, says, "As to those women on whose part ye fear disloyalty and ill conduct, admonish them, refuse to share their beds, beat them . . ." After all, she's little more than a breeding factory for future suicide bombers. You read that right.

Women are heifers for Allah.

According to published reports, Abu Hamza al-Masri, a radical Islamic cleric, urges Muslim women "to breed children for the purpose of creating suicide bombers."[19] That disdain is consistent with other female-bashing teachings from Muhammad. He had such contempt for women—aside from the obvious sexual pleasure they provided—that he wrote, "I was shown the hellfire and that the majority of its dwellers were women."[20]

Not to mention his followers are some of the worst homophobes on the planet. While lesbian practices are not mentioned directly, the Koran blasts the homosexual act: "Do ye commit lewdness such as no people in creation committed before you? For ye practice your lusts on men in preference to women: ye are indeed a people transgressing beyond bounds" (Koran 7:80-81).

According to the Hadiths—a collection of Muhammad's pearls of wisdom, compiled after his death—the prophet says, "When a man mounts another man, the throne of God shakes." What does Muhammad propose? Again, from the Hadiths, "Kill the one that is doing it and also kill the one that it is being done to."[21] Are you getting the picture? If you're a homosexual, these fanatics would stone you in a heartbeat. Period.

COMING TO AMERICA

Unlike other Muslim sects and movements, the radical followers of Muhammad who, by the way, are convinced they are the truest of believers, believe strictly in Islamic law, or sharia. Pluralistic, democratic, Western-style governments are sinful to them. Same goes for communism, socialism, or any other form of secular government. Converting the world to sharia is Job One. "Either Islam gets Europeanized," writes Bassam Tibi, a moderate Muslim and Syrian emigrant to Germany, "or Europe gets Islamized."[22]

The Islamists want the same thing here: an Islamized America. These extremists have been knocking on— and knocking *down*—America's doors for years. Sadly, the American sheeple have the attention span of a kid with ADD. Quickly forgetting the lessons of 9/11, and within just a few short months after these vermin crashed planes into the Twin Towers, the Byron

THE BYRON EXCELSIOR PUBLIC SCHOOL IN BYRON, CALIFORNIA, REQUIRED SEVENTH-GRADE STUDENTS TO PARTICIPATE IN A THREE-WEEK INTENSIVE ISLAMIC INDOCTRINATION COURSE.

Excelsior Public School in Byron, California, required seventh-grade students to participate in a three-week intensive Islamic indoctrination course.

Get this. Twelve-year-old students were "forced to pretend they were Muslims for three weeks, praying in the name of Allah the Compassionate the Merciful, chanting Praise to Allah, picking a Muslim name from a list to replace their own name and to stage their own jihad via a dice game."[23] Brainwashing, anyone?

Teachers used the *Across the Centuries* textbook created by Houghton-Mifflin along with Muslim "simulation" materials. The textbook presents Muslims as worthy of praise and imitation, but—big surprise here— "portrays Christians as intolerant persecutors of Jews and non-Christians."[24] As it turns out, the CEO of Houghton-Mifflin is from Iran,[25] which explains the intolerant bigotry and bias of their textbook.

Let me set this straight for you. American students were required to take a Muslim name, dress like a Muslim, talk like a Muslim, chant praises to Allah, and, for bonus points, memorize Muslim prayers, skip lunch to mimic fasting during Ramadan, and execute the Five Pillars of Islam!

We have a bumper crop of idiots running our schools, that's all. First, they ripped the Ten Commandments off the walls and gave God the boot.

Then they shoved condoms on cucumbers in front of our children. Now this. Can't you sheeple see the coming Islamic storm in America?

Whether you know it or not, an increasing number of our public schools are jumping on the camel, requiring their version of Islamic indoctrination. Take, for example, the students in the third, fourth, and fifth grades at the Herndon, Virginia, elementary school who will be taught the customs and practices of Islam. Columnist Alexis Amory reports, "During this instruction, public school children will play act being Muslims, and, perhaps unwittingly, convert to Islam." You might say we've gone from Reading, Writing, and Arithmetic to . . . Reading, Ritalin, and Ramadan.[26]

What's next? A Muslim Muppet on *Sesame Street?*

Why not? Why should the elementary schools have all the fun? Let's see. *Sesame Street* could introduce Omar the Butcher and his son al-Habeeb who find, beat, and cut the head off Cookie Monster for stealing food from a trash can that belonged to a Muslim seminary student. I'd say that has real possibilities in this Alice in Wonderland world that we live in.

The Islamic penetration marches on, this time dividing the close-knit, Polish-Catholic town of Hamtramck, Michigan. There, residents were forced by the Islam-influenced town council to "endure Muslim calls to prayer in Arabic broadcast over loudspeakers six times a day."[27] The Muslims claim their decree is *no different* than a Christian church signaling parishioners with church bells.

They're wrong. Church bells are a *voluntary* call to a worship which takes place behind closed doors. Imagine the uproar by the keepers of the media if Father Fred conducted mass over the loudspeakers six times a day.

Why is this happening in our schools and in our town centers? I'll tell you why. Because you're convinced Islam is about peace. Because those who speak out against Islamofascism are labeled intolerant.

Because planes don't hit our cities every day.

Because bombs aren't going off in our parking garages.

Because chemical and biological agents aren't drifting through the air like bad perfume in a cheap bordello. And because you don't really believe Muslims want to Islama-size your country.

I guess you missed the speech given by Siraj Wahaj, the *controverrrsial* New York imam, to a Muslim audience in New Jersey not long ago. He said, "If only Muslims were more clever politically, they would take over the United States and replace its constitutional government with a Caliphate [Islamic leadership body]. If we were united and strong, we would elect our own leader and give allegiance to him. Take my word, if the six to eight million Muslims unite in America, the country will come to us."[28]

To call for the overthrowing of our government is, my friend, nothing short of treason. Did I mention that Wahaj just happens to be the first Muslim to offer the daily prayer in the U.S. House of Representatives? He's a Judas in dirty holy robes. And the libs still want to give Islam a free pass? It gets worse.

While our precious children are learning the ways of the religion of peace, radical Islamists are dreaming up new techniques to stab America in the back, this time in an even more spectacular and convincing display, by whatever means available—even nuclear.

You read that correctly.

The Islamofascists are today, right now, plotting a nuclear attack on our country. According to one of the world's foremost terrorism experts, our Islamofascist enemies have the capability to do so; Yossef Bodansky is on record saying Islamic terrorists have a suitcase nuke.[29]

As I've said, one dirty bomb can ruin your whole day.

> **AS I'VE SAID,
> ONE DIRTY BOMB
> CAN RUIN YOUR WHOLE DAY.**

In spite of warnings such as this, the libs refuse to acknowledge the truth about Islamofascists: Everywhere they go, they spread war. Just look at the fifteen major religion-based conflicts in the world today. From Afghanistan to Bosnia, Chechnya to Indonesia, Kosovo to Nigeria, the Philippines to the Sudan. Every last one of them involves Muslims fighting with their neighbors. I'd like to see that fact in a Houghton-Mifflin textbook.

Instead, the liberals pray to Allah that you won't learn this lesson from history: Appeasement and playing patty-cake with radical Islam only brings more death and destruction. End of story.

THE SAVAGE SOLUTION

The fundamentalist teachings of Islam are not compatible with Western values and our Judeo-Christian heritage. This is not the fault of the West—it is due to the hatred of us by the Islamic world and its Grand Viziers of Violence and Vindictiveness. Remember, we're not the ones looking to kill or convert anybody to our way of life.

Just as Nazism, Italian fascism, and Japan's imperialist militarism were not defeated in a day, a month, or a year, neither will we obliterate this global terrorist threat overnight. The Islamists are putting in the long hours. Osama and his band of hatemongers don't take vacations at Disneyworld after a hard year creating terror. They don't rest. They keep the long view in mind: Kill or convert the infidels.

Historically speaking, Americans are not like the French. We don't run and hide behind the cover of acquiescence, nor do most of us hang around cafés sipping wine and buttering our baguettes. If 9/11 had happened in France, Jaques Chirac would have flown a white flag on the Eiffel Tower. And so, once again, we must face the threat to our survival head on.

What's the solution?

That depends on who you ask. If you're an idealistic lib who just wants to heal the world, you'd probably want us to *understaaaand* the plight of radical Islamists. So, to encourage tolerance among school students, you'd propose a Hug-a-Muslim awareness week and ban all non-Muslim religions so as not to *offeeeend* Muslim immigrants. And, to accommodate the need for frequent prayers, every student would get an official prayer rug and a hall pass to cut class and pray to Allah.

Better yet, with a donation from Hamas, we could create a "Face the Fascist" cable network and provide a mandatory subscription for every household in America. Since CNN's ratings are tanking, I'm sure Ted Turner wouldn't mind donating his studios to this worthy cause. Specialized programming like "Behind the Burka" and "My First Night with 72 Virgins" would be co-funded and produced by NPR.

Now, if you were to ask me, I'd say we need more Patton and less patent leather in Washington. On the battlefield, we must stop, disarm, or kill them before they kill us. We must be unswerving in our war on terror, both abroad and at home. Real homeland security begins when we arrest, interrogate, jail, or deport known operatives within our borders. That's number one.

> **REAL HOMELAND SECURITY BEGINS WHEN WE ARREST, INTERROGATE, JAIL, OR DEPORT KNOWN OPERATIVES WITHIN OUR BORDERS.**

What's that you say? Our jails are too crowded? Not a problem. Make room by evicting the 25 percent of prisoners who are illegal aliens. Send them back where they came from.

Second, stop pushing the Muslim faith on our children in school. Stop the brainwashing. Stop using textbooks that were created by operatives of Hamas and Hezbollah. Instead, require the czarinas of education and their sister-thought-police to present the truth as I have done in this masterpiece of outrage.

Third, treat terrorist threats as warnings rather than protected speech, and immediately investigate the threat. And don't for one second run from the use of profiling to identify terror suspects.

Fourth, going beyond the use of military force abroad (carpet-bombing the cavemen back to the Stone Age in Krapistan as needed), there has to be dialogue too, but dialogue from a credible source. In other words, the solution to this global jihad against the West must come from *moderate Muslim leaders* who preach tolerance and co-existence with the West, rather than jihad.

Take, for instance, Ahmed al-Rahim, chairman of the American Islamic Congress. On the heels of the September 11 attack, he said, "The most important message is that we condemn all kinds of hate speech including anti-Semitism and anti-Americanism and that we come out as boldly as possible against violence committed by Muslims in Iraq, in Israel, in Muslim countries like Turkey and Indonesia, and that we do all that we can in this war against terrorism."[30]

His was a rare voice of reason. Many more are needed.

> A MESSAGE OF MODERATION, NOT EXTREMISM, MUST PREVAIL IN THE ISLAMIC WORLD. WE NEED AN ARMY OF MODERATE MUSLIMS CRYING OUT, "NOT IN OUR NAME!"

Indeed, a message of moderation, not extremism, must prevail in the Islamic world. We need an army of moderate Muslims crying out, "Not in our name!" when their extremist brethren commit senseless acts of violence. Granted, we'll need to protect those moderates who have the courage to speak out against the hatemongers and bomb-tossers because of the retaliation they might suffer by their own brothers.

The good news is a movement is emerging within Islam to delegitimize its most radical elements. The Free Muslim Coalition Against Terrorism put it this way: "Muslims must look inward and put a stop to many of our religious leaders who spend most of their sermons teaching hatred, intolerance, and violent jihad. We should not be afraid to admit that . . . so many of our religious leaders belong behind bars and not behind a pulpit."[31]

When I say that moderate Islamic voices should prevail, I'm not suggesting token acts of contrition will suffice, as when the Saudi Crown Prince Abdullah telephoned Russian President Vladimir Putin after Chechen Muslim extremists seized the school in Beslan. The prince tried to assure Putin that "this terrorist act . . . goes against religious teachings and violates human and moral values."

Or when Syria's official news agency criticized that massacre as a "terrorist, cowardly action. . . ."

Or the bogus words of "grief" offered by the public relations arm of God knows who, the Council on American-Islamic Relations (CAIR): "No words can describe the horror and grief generated by the deaths of so many innocent people at the hands of those who dishonor the cause they espouse. We offer sincere condolences to the families of the victims and call for a swift resolution to the conflict in that troubled region."

These pronouncements are nothing more than "donor preservation" tactics. The statements are made to keep allies, donors, and the friendly media happy. They ring less true than campaign speeches in swing states. Notice CAIR didn't even have the courage to call the kidnappers Muslims.

Unlike CAIR, Abdel Rahman al Rashed, manager of the Al-Arabiya news channel, had the guts to be honest. He also created a stir when he said: "It is a certain fact that not all Muslims are terrorists, but it is equally certain, and exceptionally painful, that almost all terrorists are Muslims. . . ." He cited a number of incidents which involved Muslim terrorists—including

> "IT IS A CERTAIN FACT THAT NOT ALL MUSLIMS ARE TERRORISTS, BUT IT IS EQUALLY CERTAIN, AND EXCEPTIONALLY PAINFUL, THAT ALMOST ALL TERRORISTS ARE MUSLIMS."
> —ABDEL RAHMAN AL RASHED

9/11, the first World Trade Center bombing in 1993, and the daily suicide attacks against Israeli civilians. Al Rashed then asks, "Does all this tell us anything about ourselves, our societies, and our culture?"[32]

That's legitimate contrition. And he's not alone.

As recently as the fall of 2004, a dozen Arab and Islamic intellectuals met in Cairo to call for a serious reinterpretation of their various holy texts, including the Koran. Muhammad Shahrour, a layman pundit, argued that Muslims must "differentiate between the religion and state politics. When you take the political Islam, you see only killing, assassination, poisoning, intrigue, conspiracy, and civil war, but Islam as a message is very human, sensible, and just."[33]

Mr. Shahrour is particularly disturbed by the Sura of Repentance, which, he claims, has mostly to do with the prophet Muhammad's failed initiative to create a state on the Arabian Peninsula. As such, it is a violent, bloody book, which modern Islamists take out of context to justify their jihads. He and like-minded secularists, who are disgusted by the stain of Islamofascism now dominating the world stage, realize they must find a way to seize control of their faith from the fanatics if they are to have a prayer of avoiding a backlash against all Muslims.

This kind of self-examination will ultimately lead to reformation within the Muslim world. Such introspection must be encouraged. When the Muslim community takes responsibility to reign in their own people, then and only then will they demonstrate that their faith is actually a religion of peace.

If these Savage Solutions sound like a lot of work, they are. I'm well aware of the job that must be done. So, you can sit home like a moron and watch sports or porn on cable, or you can roll up your sleeves and start defending the greatest nation in the history of mankind before we're hit again. By speaking out, by watching what the schools are teaching your children, by turning off media propaganda, by calling talk radio shows.

There's no other way.

This isn't a picnic. This is a showdown.

THREE

ALIEN INVASION

A dry heat broiled the Arizona ranch like a Texas barbecue. Jake struggled to stand up, but the growing numbness in his chest strangled his ability to breathe. He pitched forward; his face mashed against the parched earth as he gasped for air. This was his land, his farm, his soil. He spent a lifetime tending to every last inch of pasture. He'd be damned if another herd of human invaders trampled his property, leaving a trail of litter and feces in their wake.

Jake rolled his neck for another look at his assailant some forty feet away. This one was different from the other two-bit bandits who breached his fences—fences like the one he was repairing when the stranger emerged from the shadows. This one had eyes of darkness, a mottled face, a black headwrap, and a thick, bushy mustache. But it was the lightning fast reflexes that struck Jake as odd. He pulled off a shot before Jake had time to react.

Military?

Not that the authorities cared. Jake had reported border violations before. Even with the flood of aliens and the bails of pot, cheap Mexican heroin, and cocaine carried in backpacks, nothing but empty promises to end the stampede ever came his way.

Jake heaved and coughed out a mouthful of blood. With a squint, he focused on the assailant. Jake inched a Colt 45 revolver from his waistband, took aim, and squeezed off two shots. Neither hit the mark.

A barrage of firepower answered his bullets. A hot, sticky pool of blood puddled beneath him, mingling with the dry dust. Jake's last thought was of Sarah, then . . .

Blackness.

Ten days after the funeral, Sarah sat in silence on the front porch swing. The memories shared with Jake during happier times embraced her like the arm of an old friend. Her bittersweet reflection was interrupted by the arrival of a late-model BMW. A middle-aged man in a tailored suit slipped out from behind the wheel.

He introduced himself as Alex from the ACLU. This was just a courtesy call, he assured her—nothing more than a desire to settle matters to avoid a trial. Sarah, he said, had been named in a lawsuit filed on behalf of Raoul Martinez of Mexico City, for her late husband's attempted murder, acts of vigilantism, and for causing emotional distress. Nine co-defendants, all non-American citizens, had joined in the suit. Alex's clients offered to settle outside of court for $3 million or, if they went to trial, he'd have no choice but to go after the entire farm.

* * *

Jake and Sarah are fictional characters, but the flood of human contraband that ranchers confront on our southern border every day is a national scandal. Worse, it's insanity. Allowing anybody—*even one person*—to sneak into America in a post 9/11 world is nothing short of suicidal. What if that illegal alien was carrying a nuclear device, sarin gas, or any number of other biowarfare agents stuffed into his backpack?

Not only are we allowing a deluge of illegals to flow across the border, we often tie the hands of the men and women whose job it is to defend our national security. As I was working on this book, I came across an article that sickened me. It's the story of Richard Gonzales, Louis Gomez, and Carlos Reyna, three U.S. Immigration officers who had made thousands of arrests without prior incident. These hard-working, uncorruptable men were fined and sentenced to jail. Their crime? They failed to give timely medical treatment to an illegal alien who had been injured during a raid.

Does it get any more upside-down than this?

U.S. District Judge Lee Rosenthal obviously has her head up her robe. This fraud refused to accept the testimony of Officer Gonzales, a veteran border agent, when he said he believed the victim was faking an injury. You've got to remember these guys see everything

> **JUDGE LEE ROSENTHAL OBVIOUSLY HAS HER HEAD UP HER ROBE.**

on the front lines—the faked injuries, the bogus excuses, the forged identities. Instead, Rosenthal sent our officers to jail. But wait, that's not all. The family of the illegal alien proceeded to sue our government in federal court and, in turn, won $2.15 million.[1]

Tell me, how an illegal alien who by definition has no right to be inside our country can be permitted to sue us?

Tell me, how would that illegal alien have been treated in his own town if he'd been caught breaking the law?

Tell me this country isn't being broken every day by the mental disorder of liberalism. People with such twisted thinking should be placed in a straightjacket.

When I say a deluge of human flotsam and jetsam are floating across our borders undetected, I'm talking about a flood of biblical proportions. Both the *Washington Times* and *Time* magazine put the figure at *more than three million* illegal aliens in 2004 alone! You better read that again. We're talking enough illegal aliens to fill "22,000 Boeing 737-700 airliners, or sixty flights every day for a year."[2]

Did you know that?

Three million illegal entries in 2004.

That's more than 8,000 *every day of the year.* And when these human invaders cross over, they disappear into the woodwork of America to gnaw away at the pillars of our society.

One day I'd like to wake up and hear any of our so-called journalists shoot straight about this crisis. Imagine the outrage if a major talking head were to announce, "Good morning everyone. Last night while you slept, 8,000 illegal aliens crossed from Mexico into America unstopped by our border agents. Today, sources at the border predict another wave of 8,000 aliens, which brings the total number of aliens entering illegally to more than three million this year."

Nor would a network spokesmouth report that there are between fifteen and twenty million illegal aliens *already living* in the United States. That's more than the estimated 2003 populations of Nevada, Oregon, and Washington combined. Some project the number to be closer to twenty million illegals, more than the entire population of Florida. Anybody want to swing an election next go 'round? Let me break this crisis down for you.

> **THERE ARE BETWEEN FIFTEEN AND TWENTY MILLION ILLEGAL ALIENS ALREADY LIVING IN THE UNITED STATES.**

HANDS ACROSS AMERICA

Take the lower number of twelve million illegals. Look at that figure this way. If you were to line up all twelve million shoulder-to-shoulder, you could form a straight line that would span from coast to coast . . . and back again. And that's with a few hundred thousand left over.[3]

Starting to get the picture?

Listen. I'm all for immigration. Over my lifetime, I'm sure I've said this at least once for every illegal in San Francisco: I'm the son of an immigrant. But there's a right and a wrong way to go about migration. What's happening to our borders is beyond disgraceful; it's a recipe for national self-destruction. Don't get all weepy with me about how these millions of illegals are just hard-working Mexicans looking to feed and deliver their impoverished families from the grinding privation of their backward homeland. I'm all for people improving their lot.

But consider this.

If three million illegal aliens can cross into our country unmolested every year, is it such a stretch to believe drug traffickers and terrorists could do the same thing? Tragically, slipping across our poorly staffed and often unmonitored border is a breeze for any narcotraffickers or terrorists seeking to avoid detection or recognition at our airports, seaports, and bus and train terminals.

Paranoia?

Scare tactics?

Hardly.

The fact of the matter is that while many illegals are hard laborers, according to an alarming report in *Time,* "190,000 illegals from countries other than Mexico have melted into the U.S. population."[4] And that's just during the first nine months of 2004. We're talking people from El

Salvador, Nicaragua, Russia, China, and Egypt, not to mention Iran and Iraq. Tell me that's not a border-sized pipeline for terrorist intruders.

In October 2004, *Washington Times* national security reporter Bill Gertz wrote about an intelligence report stating that more than two dozen members of Chechnya's Islamofanatic faction—possibly even the faction that took Russian children hostage in a school, then killed most of them before running—slipped across our wide, porous U.S.-Mexico border in Arizona in July.[5]

And these butchers are not the first batch of America haters to infiltrate our ranks. Pick up a copy of the 9/11 Commission's report, and you'll learn that a number of highly placed al-Qaida figures—the kind who trained in Afghanistan's terror spas—lived in Tucson, attended the University of Arizona, and learned to fly at area flight schools.[6]

The Grand Canyon State was (and may still be) a regular greenhouse where al-Qaida operatives planted, planned, and prepared their attack dating back to the mid-eighties. Arizona has become such a rat's nest for radical Islamic militants, the CIA and the FBI released a joint report on May 15, 2002, entitled "Arizona: Long Term Nexus for Islamic Extremist."

> PARDON THE STEREOTYPES, BUT VEGGIE-PICKERS, LEAF-BLOWERS, AND SQUEEGEE-MEN ARE ONE THING. BOMB-PLANTERS, BUILDING-BLASTERS, AND KAMIKAZES ARE SOMETHING ELSE ENTIRELY.

Other documents released to the 9/11 Commission found that Mubarak al-Duri (said to be Osama bin Laden's main procurement agent of WMDs), Wadih el Hage (convicted in the August 1998 U.S. Embassy bombing in East Africa), Hani Hanjour (the Saudi sicko who slammed a plane into the Pentagon), and Mohammed Bayazid (arms procurer for al-Qaida), all lived in and around Tucson.[7] Pardon the stereotypes, but veggie-pickers, leaf-blowers, and squeegee-men are one thing. Bomb-planters, building-blasters, and kamikazes are something else entirely. And they're already in our backyards.

Our leaders have both known and ignored this for years.

And, if you're ready for the clear evidence that liberalism is a mental disorder, instead of clamping down, our government bureaucrats are rolling out the red carpet. Take President Bush, who has called for a greater *understaaaanding* and cooperation with Mexico. Bush said, "Family values don't stop at the Rio Grande."[8] Neither do border jumpers, drug runners, or the freshman class of al-Qaida terrorists. But the president apparently filed that memo—along with our national security—in the little round file under his desk.

CHRONIC INSANITY

This ultratolerance for illegals—a by-product of liberalism—has been unchecked for decades. Not one U.S. administration since 1980 has been serious about stopping the invasion, much less controlling it. We got a glimmer of hope with President Reagan. "The simple truth is that we've lost control of our own borders," he said, "and no nation can do that and survive."[9] Then a bushel dropped on that little light of Reagan's. While his assessment was correct, the president promptly signed legislation granting amnesty to millions of illegals. Most experts agree this move led to even *more* illegal immigration, not less.

It's an old lesson of economics: You get more of what you subsidize. Concessions give birth to more concessions.

It's time to slam the door shut.

Why does America set out the welcome mat for those who subvert our

> **WHY DO WE LOOK THE OTHER WAY WHEN WE KNOW THAT NEARLY THREE QUARTERS OF THE COCAINE AND HALF OF THE HEROIN CONSUMED IN AMERICA ENTERS ACROSS THE U.S.-MEXICAN BORDER?**

immigration procedures, who snake their way across our border just to stab us in the back?

Why do we allow illegals with bogus papers to steal jobs from U.S. citizens who waited their turn and got here legally?

Why do we look the other way when we know that nearly three quarters of the cocaine and half of the heroin consumed in America enters across the U.S.-Mexican border?[10]

And speaking of drugs, here's one for you Red Doper Diaper Babies.

Did you know every year the drug cartels and their warlords stuff $500 million into the back pockets of corrupt Mexican generals for the sole purpose of buying protection from armed escorts?[11] That might explain why there have been 118 documented incursions by the Mexican military just in the last five years.[12] Far too often our border agents face fully-armed, Mexican military personal driving Hummers acting as a personal valet service for drug mules. This is reason enough to use our military to shut down the border, which we'd do if we were serious about America's drug war.

Which begs the question, why doesn't the president at least call out the National Guard to stop this threat to our health, welfare, and security? I've got news for you. Neither Republicans nor Democrats *want to stop the flow*. Why? It's a little cynical, but one Cochise County sheriff who works the border put it this way: "People in Washington get up in the morning, their laundry is done, their floors are cleaned, their meals are cooked. Guess who's doing that?"[13]

A little cynicism will keep you healthy.

While America had her shirts pressed, her floors washed, and her food cooked, the guys on the front lines—the U.S. Border Patrol with the thankless job of defending our southern flank—nabbed 55,890 illegal OTMs (Other Than Mexican aliens) from October 2003 to August 2004.[14] Those were just the ones who got caught. And these U.S. Border Patrol agents, who now must carry guns and who are vastly outnumbered by the aliens, say they are lucky if they can catch one in five illegal crossers.[15]

So, who's to blame?

Hypocritical politicians on the political left and right, that's who. Their negligence is inexcusable. Article IV, Section 4 of the U.S. Constitution says,

The United States shall guarantee to every state in this union, a republican form of government, and *shall protect each of them against invasion* (my emphasis).

Thanks to their failure to follow the Constitution with the same fervor with which they slavishly follow poll numbers, our borders are more porous than your grandmother's sieve.

What's worse is that since April 2004 border agents have been forced to *release* most illegal aliens back onto American streets within hours of catching them—even when some of them are known criminals or are from countries known to produce terrorists.[16] Whatever for?

Budget cuts.

Great. We've got money for abortion education. We've got foreign-aid dollars for Iraqis and Palestinians. We've even got bucks for AmeriCorps to plant trees for Earth Day. So why not this? *Oh, I forgot.* Because we're so sensitive, we've got to reserve tax dollars to subsidize the ever popular, annual gay pride celebration for federal employees.[17] At least our priorities are straight.

JAILHOUSE ROCK

Once again our brilliant leaders have dropped the ball. Which explains why about a dozen illegal aliens from several "countries of special interest" (which is nothing more than a politically sanitized code phrase for "terrorist-sponsoring nation") were captured near the New York and Vermont borders but then were cut loose. We're talking about aliens from Pakistan and Morocco.[18] Says T.J. Bonner of the Border Patrol Agents Association, "It's simply mind-numbing to the agents. We catch people who could possibly be terrorists and we're being told, 'Gee, we're out of money, we have to let them go.'"[19]

Writer Frosty Wooldridge observed: "John Slagle, a former thirty-year Border Patrol officer, noted last year that, among 37,000 captured illegal aliens in the Tucson, Arizona, sector, 7,500 were from terror-sponsoring countries. Since they only catch one in four, what if the ones that got into the USA gained driver's licenses? How about another 9/11 brought to you by your leaders. How do you think we suffered the first one?"[20]

And, according to Democrat Congressman Solomon P. Ortiz, who sits on the House Armed Services Subcommittee on Readiness, a number of Middle Easterners were detained and then released after coming to America at the Mexican border. Why? Although they had possible ties to terrorist groups, the jails were already full. Ortiz said, "It is true. It is very reliable information, from the horse's mouth, and it's happening all over the place. It's very, very scary, and members [of Congress] know about this."[21]

At least Democrat Senator Zell Miller shoots straight with us—not that his spineless peers were listening. Miller labeled the illegal alien problem nothing short of "a bipartisan dereliction of duty."[22] You see, those who have the power to stop the insanity only offer us lip service. Why?

They don't want to lose a few votes. Period.

Says Miller, "Not the executive branch, not the legislative branch, not diplomats, not business, not labor, not educators, not farmers, not religious leaders, and especially not Democratic or Republican lawmakers . . . it has become a high stakes contest between the leaders of both parties to see which one can pander the most."[23]

There's another aspect of this national nightmare about which our leaders, once again, are spineless: What should be done with the millions of illegal aliens who have already entered America? You see, there are two parts to the problem—first, stopping the hordes who are jumping the border even as you read these words; and second, dealing with those who have already disappeared into our population, assuming we can find them.

Ah, now there's the politically incorrect rub. When the Census Bureau attempts to count illegal aliens, they don't answer the door. When an illegal alien is required to attend a deportation hearing they, more often than not, fail to show up. No surprise there.

And, whenever law enforcement officers seek to conduct broad sweeps of the Hispanic community to round 'em up and ship 'em out—mind you, not just along the border, but in communities across the country, as well they should—various socialist front groups like the ACLU sue to stop these legitimate efforts at national survival.

So, if we can't find them, by default the illegal alien lives the American dream, often times tax-free and at the taxpayers expense.

Granted, some argue we don't have enough agents in the first place even if we had the will to do the job. There are fewer than 2,000 federal agents to handle the momentous job of "interior

> THERE ARE FEWER THAN 2,000 FEDERAL AGENTS TO HANDLE THE MOMENTOUS JOB OF "INTERIOR ENFORCEMENT," NAMELY, TO ROUND UP AND DEPORT ALIEN INVADERS.

enforcement," namely, to round up and deport alien invaders.[24] It's precisely this lack of interior enforcement that entices Mexican border jumpers to risk life and limb, to stuff themselves in the trunks of cars, to piggyback a ride on a northbound freight train or—and this is unbelievable to me—to be welded inside of ship cargo units.[25]

You know what drives me crazy on this issue?

Think back to the mad cow disease scare. I remember when Canada learned they had one sick cow. Somehow health department officials in our government were able to track down that cow to a stall in Washington State. They can locate one sick cow but can't find where fifteen million illegal aliens are grazing in our country. Most creative solution I've heard so far: Give every illegal a bovine buddy so we can keep better track of him.[26]

KEYS TO THE PROMISED LAND:
HEALTH, EDUCATION, WELFARE

What should be done about those who are here? Zell Miller says our leaders "should muster up the will to send illegal aliens back to where they came from. Instead, both parties stumble all over themselves to grant amnesty."[27]

And driver's licenses.

And Medicare.

And school lunches.

And college grants.

And you the sheeple get to foot the bill.

For their part, the hybrid-driving libs sound so high and mighty and compassionate as they reach around to pick your pocket. Never mind the fact that when an illegal alien refuses to pay taxes and yet still benefits from a full menu of social services, they're bankrupting the system.

In the emerging New America, one without borders, socialist liberals ask you to walk a mile in the illegal's poncho. Can you blame them for coming here to earn ten bucks an hour under the table, the libs say, when the most these souls can earn in Mexico is sixty cents a day?

Whether we can "blame" these invaders is not really the point. The

> **THE HYBRID-DRIVING LIBS SOUND SO HIGH AND MIGHTY AND COMPASSIONATE AS THEY REACH AROUND TO PICK YOUR POCKET.**

point is that while the left plays on the sympathy and generosity of the American people, America is being bled dry. Many schools in states with huge illegal populations are being destroyed; hospitals are bankrupt and are closing; and the legal bills in many communities devour tax dollars earmarked for capital improvements.

Hard to believe?

Go visit a hospital in one of our border states.

Pay special attention to what's going on in the emergency room. The situation is so touchy some nurses actually carry side arms.[28] The illegals—some of whom arrive by taxi directly from Mexico—line the walls, crowding you out, demanding Spanish interpreters and free medical care even as the American citizens who actually foot the bill are denied.

Come to think of it, save your pesos and forget about the taxis. Mexican *ambulances* routinely bring uninsured Mexican patients across the border to U.S. hospitals. An article in the *Washington Times* cites U.S. authorities as saying, "The border crossings have been reported from Brownsville, Texas, to Douglas, Arizona, and involve Mexican ambulance companies whose drivers have been instructed by hospital officials in Mexico to take ailing and uninsured patients to the United States."[29]

All of this costs U.S. hospitals in the neighborhood of $200 million a year and more.[30] Those that can, pay the tab; so many others, however, can't and therefore are closing their doors. In 2000, San Diego's Scripps Memorial Hospital was forced to close because it was losing $5 million a year, mostly due to having to provide care to illegal aliens that was not reimbursed.[31]

Complicating the picture is the exodus of doctors. Border-area hospitals report that they are short physicians and surgeons because these skilled professionals left for positions where their salaries were not tied to a mass of illegal aliens who skip out on their bills.[32]

> **TREATING UNINSURED ILLEGAL ALIENS COSTS ABOUT $2.2 BILLION A YEAR.**

Bottom line? According to the Center for Immigration Reform, treating uninsured illegal aliens costs about $2.2 billion a year.[33]

If that doesn't make you sick, how about this gem: Hospitals are going broke in Texas, New Mexico, Arizona, and California because they are forced to subsidize Mexico's poorest people,[34] and because—you're not going to believe it when I tell you—hospitals must absorb "the costs of providing federally mandated emergency-room services to illegal aliens *injured crossing the border*"[35] (my emphasis).

Here's another shocker: In early October 2004, Health and Human Resources Secretary Tommy Thompson announced that American tax dollars were being spent *in Mexico* in medical clinics. For what? To provide Mexicans prenatal care! At least Thompson, while making his announcement, was honest enough to say, "Well, we're doing this because if we can prevent illness down there they won't bring it here."[36]

America may be north of the border, but this isn't the North Pole and we're not Santa. Our constitutional obligation is *not* to swoop down into every mud hut across the globe dropping gold-plated medical and educational packages. Our obligation is to maintain the integrity of our borders, language, and culture for our own citizens.

Dick Gephardt evidently likes his role as St. Nick. With "Jingle Bells" playing in the background, Gephardt had this to say about illegal aliens: "If children are here, they have to be educated. They have to get basic health care. And the federal government needs to fill some of that need."[37] Show me that provision in our Constitution, Dick.

NO ALIEN LEFT BEHIND

Regarding education, take a morning drive to any port of entry along our border with Mexico during the school year. What will you see? Try scores of Mexican children crossing our borders, often in sight of immigration and Border Patrol agents who are prohibited from detaining them. Backpacks in hand, these students come to American schools because they can't get a decent education in their own country.

In fact, each year "65,000 undocumented students [read: illegal aliens] graduate from our nation's high schools."[38] Did you know that, as of 1996, it cost about $8 billion a year just to provide a primary education for illegal aliens at the federal, state, and local levels?[39] Who pays for that? The Mexican government?

> **IT'S ALL PART OF THE NO ILLEGAL ALIEN LEFT BEHIND PROGRAM.**

Sorry, Señor. You do and I do—even as our schools panhandle for teachers, supplies, and much-needed resources to modernize aging buildings and outdated technology. It's all part of the No Illegal Alien Left Behind program.

And there's more.

Let's not forget to factor in Medicaid and welfare handouts to the children of illegal aliens. I realize most adult illegals don't get Medicaid or welfare because they tend to avoid any and all contact with the federal government. But their children do—especially those born in the United States. Why? How do their children qualify?

I'll tell you. According to the Fourteenth Amendment to the U.S. Constitution:

> All persons born or naturalized in the United States, and subject to the jurisdiction thereof, are citizens of the United States and of the state wherein they reside.

Bet you forgot that one. Funny how the illegals, who can't read English, somehow know this. Which explains why tens of thousands sneak into our country every year to have their babies: So-called U.S. citizen babies are then entitled to other taxpayer-supplied government benefits. And, when they turn twenty-one, they can sponsor the immigration of other relatives, becoming "anchor babies" for each clan.[40]

And when I say they "sneak" into our country, I'm talking on foot, by horse, by car, by train, by truck, in a storage container, and stuffed into every imaginable place including the four-year-old who was sealed inside of a piñata.[41] They'll stop at nothing to shoehorn their way into America.

In a nutshell, using the most current figures, here's what illegal aliens and their children cost U.S. taxpayers on an annual basis just at the federal level:

- $2.1 billion to lock up illegals in prisons;[42]
- $2.5 billion in Medicaid;
- $2.2 billion in uninsured medical costs;
- $1.4 billion in federal aid to schools;
- $1.9 billion in food stamps, WIC, and free school lunches.[43]

Now, the next time you get paid, take a hard, long look at your pay stub. Focus on the column where it says "Federal Income Taxes Withheld." That's the money you *earned* but don't get to keep. Then remember this: A portion of the cash the government has taken from your wallet is paying for that $10 billion handout.

PEDAL TO THE METAL

If I had to pick one of the dumbest things local, state, and some federal leaders are pushing for, it has to be the race to issue driver's licenses to illegal aliens. We all know Congresswoman Carol Moseley-Braun is off her rocker. But get a load of this tripe from the Democratic representative: "Those who live here ought to be able to get a driver's license, ought to be able to participate as citizens participate. We need to normalize our relations with documented, as well as undocumented people who are here in the U.S."

And people vote for this woman? How can she utter such garbage and be reelected?

It gets worse. In her upside-down world, "It doesn't matter if you came to this country on the Mayflower or a slave ship, across the Rio Grande or through Ellis Island, we are all in the same boat now."[44] I take it she's not familiar with the Illegal Immigration Reform and Immigrant Responsibility Act, which states that "stowaways, regardless of when encountered, are to be removed without a hearing" (Section 235[a][2]).

If it were up to me, the only car they'd ever ride in would be the back of a police van headed to the nearest deportation center. Before you call me a racist xenophobic vigilante, let me tell you why I am so strident on this issue. A driver's license gives terrorists greater flexibility to blend in with the rest of us. With it, they can rent storage units to store weapons, rent houses, board airplanes, and open credit card and bank accounts. All quite useful things when looking to attack Americans on our own soil.

Did you know that two of the 9/11 hijackers had valid Virginia driver's licenses? Did you know that Mohammed Atta, one of the 9/11 masterminds, was stopped by a policeman but wasn't detained because he possessed and displayed a valid license—even though he was, essentially, an illegal alien with an expired visa? Virginia has since rescinded that idiotic law, but try comforting the survivors of the victims of 9/11 with that.

> DID YOU KNOW THAT MOHAMMED ATTA, ONE OF THE 9/11 MASTERMINDS, WAS STOPPED BY A POLICEMAN BUT WASN'T DETAINED BECAUSE HE POSSESSED AND DISPLAYED A VALID LICENSE—EVEN THOUGH HE WAS, ESSENTIALLY, AN ILLEGAL ALIEN WITH AN EXPIRED VISA?

Meantime, upwards of fourteen states still issue illegal aliens driver's licenses.[45] Who would do something so stupid, so careless, so suicidal after the worst terrorist attacks on our own soil in U.S. history? Try Governor John Balducci of Maine, or Governor Janet Napolitano of Arizona, or New York City Mayor Michael Bloomberg, for starters. Even Governor Jeb Bush, the president's own brother, backed efforts in his home state of Florida to provide illegals licenses.[46]

If common sense won't prevail, you'd think these leaders would at the very least know it's against federal law to provide "aid and comfort" to alien invaders. Section 8 of the United States Code, 1324 (a)(1)(A)(iv)(b)(iii) says, "A person (including a group of persons, business, organization, or local government) commits a federal felony when she or he: assists an illegal alien she/he should reasonably know is illegally in the U.S. . . . or knowingly assists illegal aliens due to personal convictions."

Isn't providing illegals with driver's licenses "knowingly" assisting them?

Thankfully, the lawmakers in Tennessee saw the headlights and reversed their move to dole out licenses without proof of citizenship.

IDENTITY CRISIS

While I'm on the topic about personal identification, think back to the time when you were an underage teenager with your hat on backwards. Did you ever try to get into a club that served alcohol using a fake ID? In a way, that's what's happening these days. Tens of thousands of illegal aliens from Mexico routinely try to get into the U.S. and then stay for extended periods of time using phony identification cards available from any one of the dozens of Mexican consulate offices in America.

Have you heard of these?

They're called *"matricula consular* cards." They're available for purchase by illegal aliens to provide them with "identification" while milking the system in America. Of course, the Mexican government denies that *matricula consular* cards are a means to subvert U.S. immigration law. But tell me this: If immigrants are here in our country legally, they'd have their own U.S.-issued paperwork; they wouldn't *need* a Mexico-issued ID card.

Yet scores of Mexican illegals have them. Between 2002 and 2003, Mexico issued 2.2 million of these bogus IDs.[47] And with them, illegals are accessing U.S. banks[48] and a host of other services offered by a growing number of American cities across the country. And, while the FBI is concerned that such cards can facilitate a variety of crimes including money laundering and masking an alien's true identity from authorities, while enjoying the freedom of moving around in our country, nothing has been done to prohibit their widespread acceptance.

Here's the irony. In Mexico, the official ID is your voter registration card. According to columnist Allan Wall, a U.S. citizen who lives and works in Mexico, Mexican banks don't even accept the *matricula consular* card![49]

Not surprisingly, other countries are following suit.

You've got to keep in mind that most nations in Central and South America are poorer than dirt. Now, if you were the leader of an impoverished Central or South American country and you knew you could export your biggest social problem—poverty—to Santa in the north, wouldn't you do it? To them, printing these ID cards is like printing money. In their view, exporting poverty sure beats having to feed, clothe, and house the unwashed, impoverished masses of their countries.

> IF YOU WERE THE LEADER OF AN IMPOVERISHED CENTRAL OR SOUTH AMERICAN COUNTRY AND YOU KNEW YOU COULD EXPORT YOUR BIGGEST SOCIAL PROBLEM—POVERTY— TO SANTA IN THE NORTH, WOULDN'T YOU DO IT?

By the way, here's today's Blue Light Special for any and all illegal aliens who sign up for a *matricula consular* card. You can now use that ID to obtain a driver's license from the Department of Motor Vehicles in the state of North Carolina.[50] That's why I call the DMV the Department of Mexican Voters.

WHAT'S IN A NAME?

But the real outrage is this:Illegal aliens have become the new privileged class. This, to me, is the defining issue. The hard-left has hoodwinked Americans into being so politically correct, so globally minded, and so self-loathing of our nationalism, we the sheeple no longer demand that our elected officials defend our borders. As I've been saying for over a decade, a nation is defined by her borders, language, and culture.

Which is why I say shame on Mexican President Vicente Fox. Instead of honoring our mutual border, he actually encourages willing Mexicans to "seek work in the United States,"[51] while calling for "a fully open border within ten years, with 'a free flow of people, workers' moving between the two countries."[52]

Naturally, the lunatic fringe on the left (and right) stands up and cheers without studying the fine print.

Do you have any idea what the illegal aliens (I'm talking about those from Mexico) are doing with their cash? Sending their money south of the border—a whopping $13 billion in 2003. In fact, those funds represent "the third largest source of revenue in Mexico's economy, trailing only oil and manufacturing."[53]

Rather than work at the difficult task of jamming thirteen million fat fingers in the leaky dyke, President Bush took the easy route and stepped in it with this line: "Remember, we've got hardworking citizens who are willing to walk 400 miles of desert in blistering heat to find work."[54]

Did you catch what Bush just did?

Like many before him on the political left, Bush failed to stand up for the American worker while conducting "reassignment surgery" on the meaning of words. Go back and reread what he said: "We've got hard-working *citizens* . . ." Citizens? To me they are *illegal aliens*. With a Karl Rovian stroke of the tongue, Bush changed the status of illegals, at least in the minds of the sheeple. He's not alone; nor did he start this trend toward reassignment surgery on the English language.

Not to be upstaged, Dick Gephardt called illegal aliens "*very* good citizens."[55] Of course, I have to wonder how Gephardt knows these folks are "very good" if we can't find them. A minor point, I'm sure. Wesley Clark referred to illegal aliens simply as "undocumented workers."[56] That would be like calling a burglar who crawled through a window into your home an "undocumented house guest."

These men are playing David Copperfield with the law, making it disappear before our eyes. In the fight to preserve our sovereignty and national

> **THAT WOULD BE LIKE CALLING A BURGLAR WHO CRAWLED THROUGH A WINDOW INTO YOUR HOUSE AN "UNDOCUMENTED HOUSE GUEST."**

identity, let's not mince words. We're facing the worst betrayal of our country in our lifetime.

JAIL BIRDS, NOT PEOPLE

Just to show you how upside down our national security priorities are, the U.S. Fish & Wildlife Service and the U.S. Immigration and Customs Enforcement (ICE) were praised for their amazing job capturing a group of smugglers. These dangerous sneaks were caught trying to cross the border into San Diego with a lethal cargo. What were they attempting to smuggle?

Chemical weapons? Arms? Illegal militants?

Answer: Birds.

Probably inspired by George Bush's passage of a new "get tough" legislation to seal the border, the ICE patrol put the freeze on illegal *birds*. Not jailbirds, mind you. ICE prevented the migration of 150 Lilac Crowned and Mexican Redhead Amazon parrots. A spokesperson from WildAid, whose name isn't important, said, "The illegal bird trade causes the death of hundreds of thousands of birds, threatens some with extinction, and poses a serious risk of disease . . ."[57]

Let's stop right there. Last time I checked we were at war with Islamofascism, not the parrot kingdom. And these bird brains are worried about the potential deaths of smuggled birds? What about the risk we the American people face when militants from al-Qaida fly across the border?

He goes on: "We call upon Congress to put more resources into the USFWS to stop this illegal wildlife trade and to protect the Nation's human health and agriculture from disease." What about protecting the country's health by averting a terrorist attack? We don't have enough border guards to prevent the flood of illegal aliens from swamping our shores, but we're supposed to stop the flow of illegal parrots? Once again liberalism flocks to the wrong side of the issue.

> **LAST TIME I CHECKED WE WERE AT WAR WITH ISLAMOFASCISM, NOT THE PARROT KINGDOM.**

STABBED IN THE BACK

In a shameless display of Vicente Fox's disregard for America's borders, Mexico's Foreign Ministry created and began distributing 1.5 million copies of a new comic book-like primer packed with advice for Mexican border jumpers in December 2004. The booklet states: "This guide is intended to give you some practical advice that could be of use if you have made the difficult decision to seek new work opportunities outside your country."[58]

This colorful, easy to understand booklet is being distributed throughout the five Mexican states from which most illegal aliens herald: Puebla, Oaxaca, Michoacan, Zacatecas, and Jalisco. The booklet spells out "safety tips" for crossing the desert ("Try to walk during times when the heat is not as intense"), what to do if stopped by a border guard ("Raise your arms slowly so they see you are unarmed"), and recommends caution when working with *coyotes*—immigrant smugglers.

Four pages explain how to blend in and live peaceably in the United States ("Avoid attracting attention, at least while you are arranging your stay or documents to live in the United States"), and a full seven pages outline the migrants' rights if detained by what appear to be stern-faced border patrol agents. Rights?

Since when does a criminal have rights?

Listen to the doublespeak from Elizabeth Garcia Mejia, a spokes-chick from the migrant protection service. She claims, "We are not inviting them to cross, but we're doing everything we can to save lives." I don't buy it. If what she says were the case, the best way to save lives is for Vicente Fox to encourage Mexican citizens to seek *legal* forms of immigration. And yet this booklet provides *not one* line of information about how to obtain a U.S. visa or how to initiate legal migration.

Instead of providing Mexicans with the resources to follow the law and migrate legally, this booklet explains how to safely cross rivers: "Thick clothing increases your weight when wet, and this makes it difficult to swim or float." Sadly, the mental disorder of liberalism has warped the thinking of at least one border agent who actually thinks this resource might be a good thing. Andy Adame, a spokesman in the Border Patrol's Tucson sector, said, "If they've already gone ahead and made that decision to cross illegally . . . then anything that helps protect lives is worth it."[59]

> THE BEST WAY TO SAVE LIVES IS FOR VICENTE FOX TO ENCOURAGE MEXICAN CITIZENS TO SEEK LEGAL FORMS OF IMMIGRATION. AND YET THIS BOOKLET PROVIDES NOT ONE LINE OF INFORMATION ABOUT HOW TO OBTAIN A U.S. VISA OR HOW TO INITIATE LEGAL MIGRATION.

Using Andy's classic liberal logic, what's next? I guess we should provide blankets, canteens, compasses, maps, flashlights, and first-aid kits, too. Guess what? Certain insane liberal do-goodys do just that and provide condoms, too!

THE SAVAGE SOLUTION

If I were a good liberal, I might eliminate the problem by annexing Mexico. Let's become one happy Mexi-American family. Who needs borders, anyway? Borders divide, love unites. Then we'd dismantle the patrols and retrain former agents to serve as the Welcoming Committee. They'd hand out maps, ACLU membership cards, and visitor passes to Disneyland. During our Grand Opening, how about offering the kiddies free tattoos . . .

But I'm not a good liberal. I'm not even a bad one.

What's it going to take for you to picket the halls of Congress and demand that they stop this invasion? A small plane filled with C-4 plastic explosives flown into a crowded football field? A biohazard outbreak in your drinking water? Or maybe after the terrorist infiltrators (who trained in Arizona) begin to blow up our theaters, shopping malls, grocery stores, or, God forbid, the school where your children are enrolled? Al-Qaida is ready and willing to help out here. Isn't the bankruptcy of several states sufficient to demand action?

So, where do we begin?

First, beef up border security. By executive order, the president must immediately dispatch our military to stop the swarm. Pull our troops out of Europe, Korea, or other nations where they are doing little more than policing the locals and redeploy them to defend our homeland security. That's number one.

At the very least, call up the reservists to help man the Cyclopes; these portable, hydraulic guard booths have already been purchased and placed in service on the border. However, many remain empty due to a shortage of manpower. Likewise, millions of dollars are being spent to place *traffic cameras* in our major cities to fight crime. Employ the same technology on the border. Toss in satellite detection systems, and create a national database of border jumpers' fingerprints to aid in enforcement.

Second, end the handouts. Illegal aliens must get the memo that Santa is dead. That means if you're not an American citizen (or here on a valid student or work visa), you can't use our hospitals, you can't attend our schools, you can't receive benefits, you can't use Mexican IDs, and you most certainly cannot vote in our elections. In other words, you remove the incentive for them to remain in our country.

Don't believe for one second that we'll have nobody to pick our crops, cut our yards, or work the slaughterhouses if we drive the illegals out. I know how hard those workers work and how they're willing to put in the long hours in the hot sun. I am not a blind man. I drive through the central valley of California; I see them picking vegetables in the scorching heat. It's murder.

But guess what? There were vegetable pickers long before the illegals got here. How were the grapes picked? Go read John Steinbeck's *The Grapes of Wrath.* They were picked by Oklahomans whose farms got wiped out in the wind storms. They came out in their broken trucks and harvested the fields. They were the "migrant" workers of the past.

The poor blacks did it. The poor whites did it. As they did back then, the underclass in America—excuse me, the "emerging class"—could do that work. Why don't they pick the tomatoes today? I'll tell you. They're not motivated. They're handed welfare and food stamps. If you take away the magnet of getting something for just sitting on your behind, they'd *have* to pick the grapes, clean the toilets, and work in the slaughterhouses, that's all.

Third, simply enforce the laws. In 1986, Congress passed the Immigration Reform and Control Act, which provided fines of ten grand per illegal for businesses who imported or hired aliens. Likewise, as stated earlier in the chapter, numerous provisions covering the deportation of illegals and stowaways are already on the books and must be used to eject those illegals in our midst who live in the shadows.

Fourth, kick illegals out of our prisons. Why in the world are we clothing, feeding, housing, and providing cable TV for illegal aliens in what are already overcrowded jails? Using the latest available figures, the total prison population as of December 2002 was 2,166,260 inmates.[60] Of that, 29 percent are illegal aliens—or, put another way, nearly three in ten of the prisoners who are incarcerated don't even belong in our country. The hardest hit states are California, New York, Texas, Florida, Arizona, and New Jersey, in that order.[61]

What does this cost you and me? On average, $2 billion is spent each year to incarcerate illegal immigrants at the state, county, and city level.[62] This must end.

Fifth, launch Operation Alien Airlines. Round up all illegal aliens (take the low number of 12 million) and fly them home. If you calculate the high cost per ticket at $250, that comes to $3 billion—little more than it costs to provide Medicaid benefits to the children of illegal aliens for one year.[63] I'm sure United, Delta, and USAIR wouldn't mind the extra business. And it might keep them from falling into bankruptcy.

There is even precedence for this. In 1954, the United States Immigration Service began the politically insensitive but effective "Operation Wetback" in Texas, which, by year's end, resulted in the deportation or repatriation to Mexico of 1.3 million illegal aliens, according to government statistics.[64]

Now, before I give you the centerpiece of the Savage Solution, I'm aware there are a host of other ways to keep aliens out, not the least of which is pressuring the Mexican government to offer their people an incentive to stay home. A living wage comes to mind.

That said, I envision an *Oil for Illegals* program. They have what we want (oil), and we have something they don't want (aliens). Here's how the program will work. In order to help offset the expenses America incurs from this alien invasion and to keep energy costs low for American consumers, the president should demand one barrel of oil from Mexico for every illegal alien in our country.

Our southern neighbor is the third-largest exporter of oil to the U.S., but it's the primary "exporter" of illegal aliens to our country—as noted above, that figure is in excess of three million illegals in 2004. Mexico's proven oil reserves are estimated to be 15.7 billion barrels, the fourth-largest in the Western Hemisphere after Canada, Venezuela, and the U.S. Factor in condensate, natural gas liquids, and refinery gain with crude oil reserves, that total rises to 40.6 billion barrels.[65]

> **THE PRESIDENT SHOULD DEMAND ONE BARREL OF OIL FROM MEXICO FOR EVERY ILLEGAL ALIEN IN OUR COUNTRY.**

Mexico exports most of its excess crude through Pemex, one of the world's largest oil companies, or about 1.75 million barrels a day. The U.S. imports *most* of that, or about 1.6 million barrels per day.[66]

If three million illegals come north, we get three million barrels of oil for free. What's fair is fair. The payment, of course, would decline as we seal the border. Then again, the American people are owed tens of billions of dollars in *reparations from Mexico* for feeding, clothing, and providing health care for millions of illegal aliens over the last several decades.

Stay focused for another half second. We've been attacked on our own soil. Thousands of our brothers and sisters died in cold blood. And yet we've left the backdoor wide open for an encore. German philosopher Hegel said, "We learn from history that we never learn anything from history." For the sake of your children, your grandchildren, and all that's good in this country, you better pray to God he's wrong.

Defending our borders is the *only* way to defend the sovereignty of America. This is *the* seminal issue of our time. Mark my words, either we get control of our border, or America disappears into the melting pot of the New World Order, amalgamated as one more socialist entity answering to the United Nations.

FOUR

TRADERS VS. TRAITORS

The venomous left has ratcheted up their attacks upon the fabric of our society unlike anything I have seen in my entire lifetime. Like the pit vipers that they are, they're injecting their poison into the backbone of society: our system of free enterprise.

Whether you own your own business or work for a corporation, the traitors on the left, specifically the Red Diaper Doper Babies, have unleashed the Briefcase Mafia. These trial lawyers, along with the self-serving, socialist-leaning Demoncats and the turncoat Republicans, are working in tandem to intimidate, regulate, tax, and sue the "traders"—the hard-working people who own businesses—out of existence.

As capitalists, we're a nation of producers, entrepreneurs, and dreamers. Americans have spawned more advances in science, medicine, technology, agriculture, manufacturing, space exploration, and film than any country in the history of the world. Our innovation is largely a byproduct of the profit motive inherent in our system of capitalism. Unlike socialism, financial rewards and personal gratification await those who work hard, take risks, and invest wisely.

> USING PREDATORY LITIGATION AND OPPRESSIVE REGULATION, THESE TRAITORS ASSAIL THE BUSINESSES THAT MAKE OUR COUNTRY STRONG, THAT FUEL OUR ECONOMY, THAT PAVE A HIGHWAY TO THE FUTURE WITH DREAMS OF A BETTER DAY.

However, neo-socialist lefties hate capitalism.

Using predatory litigation and oppressive regulation, these traitors assail the businesses that make our country strong, that fuel our economy, that pave a highway to the future with dreams of a better day. As you'll see in a moment, it's as though the left's disgust for the American way of life has been plugged up like a clogged sewer, and now they've unleashed a flood of frivolous litigation and Gestapo-ish tactics to wreak havoc on American employers, costing them time, money, and jobs.

The cartel of radical forces on the left, and their accomplices on the right with their obsession with "free trade," have made the cost of doing business difficult for the small-business owner. In an attempt to stay solvent, many employers are forced to cut jobs, raise prices, alter product lines, outsource work overseas, and, failing those measures, declare bankruptcy.

THE "GUAC" THICKENS

Before I chronicle what the left is doing to drive a dagger through the heart of American businesses, let me be clear about something. These days there's little difference between the "Demicans" and the "Republicrats." When I first voted for George W. Bush, I didn't think I was getting Bill Clinton-lite: all the trade and immigration policies of the left without the sexaphonics!

The way Bush's policies headed after his reelection, I have to wonder what the man is thinking. John Kerry had barely conceded when the Bush administration took a hard, left turn. Evidently infected by the mental disorder of liberalism, Bush immediately embraced a number of programs catering to foreign interests while placing our homegrown businesses at great risk for their survival.

> **WHEN I FIRST VOTED FOR GEORGE W. BUSH, I DIDN'T THINK I WAS GETTING BILL CLINTON-LITE.**

Case in point: the avocado industry.

For the first time in ninety years, the United States Department of Agriculture under the direct hand of George Bush announced it would lift the ban against importing avocados from Mexico into California. Why is that an issue, you may ask? Inviting Mexican growers to dump their produce in America's supermarkets further devastates California's already suffering economy.

Estimates place the loss in crop sales to California growers at 20 percent annually. Which means while you enjoy guacamole from avocados fertilized with human fecal matter (as they do south of the border), California's agriculture revenue is seriously diminished by this pandering to Mexico. Why would Mr. Bush do this to our farmers?

Just as there's no such thing as a free lunch, there's no such thing as free trade. Less revenue equals fewer jobs for American workers. That's evidently one lesson Gov. Arnold Schwarzenegger hasn't learned. The minute Bush's plan to give away a fifth of the avocado business hit the wires, Arnold should have jumped on the back of a Hummer with a bullhorn and shouted: "No way, Hombre! It's U.S. avocados all the way."

If Schwarzenegger, who, I might add, appears preoccupied with changing the U.S. Constitution so he can run for president, and the two phony senators in empty skirts from California keep a button on their lips, then they deserve to be thrown out on their sombreros. How can they have nothing to say when an indigenous industry like this is going down the toilet because Bush wants "free trade"?

What can be more sacred than the family farm?

Am I the only one who sees how this move puts the screws to the American farmers? Sure, prices for avocados might drop a few pennies at the market. But let me tell you something. A lot more than cheap avocados is at stake here. There are 6,500 California avocado growers, many of whom are family farms that have been in business for a hundred years. Because George Bush caved to the Mexican farmers, these family businesses are getting eaten alive.

Before you dismiss me as a nationalist who doesn't like the idea of outsourcing jobs to Mexico, which I don't, keep in mind that the entire avocado industry is getting smashed because foreigners are being allowed to dump their inferior, pesticide-contaminated produce on our shores.

Did I mention Bush's timing couldn't be worse?

For the first time since 1959, America is experiencing a *negative* balance on agricultural trade. Put another way, we're allowing other countries to sell more of their produce here than we export abroad. Bob Schramm, a produce industry lobbyist, said, "We have signed all these free-trade agreements with countries that export to the United States but provide very few market opportunities for us."[1]

> **NAME ONE BUSINESS THAT CAN SURVIVE IF WE GIVE AWAY OUR MARKETS TO FOREIGN INTERESTS.**

Name one business that can survive if we give away our markets to foreign interests. Why, then, is the Bush administration hell-bent on undermining these American farmers? Who's advising him to do this? Frankly, I'd expect this kind of hoodwink from the Dems, but from the Republicans? Like I said, you can't tell the two parties apart these days. Believe it or not, this gets worse.

Not only did George Bush—the King of Outsourcing—invite Mexican producers to take a giant bite out of our agriculture market, resulting in the heavy loss of jobs to American workers, he's working overtime to lower the wages of the poorest of workers with his so-called "guest-worker" program. When he first proposed rewarding illegal aliens from Mexico with legal status in January of 2004, I figured Bush was just trying to capture the Hispanic vote.

But after he was reelected, Bush continued to push ahead with the granting of amnesty to illegal workers. He lost no time sending the Three Amigos, Colin Powell, Tom Ridge, and Norman Mineta, to Mexico to discuss the merits and details of his initiative. Powell assured Mr. Fox that the Bush administration was committed to making progress on the issue of migration.

MEMO TO PRESIDENT BUSH: *You won the election already; stop trying to secure the Hispanic vote.*

In my view, granting guest-worker passes would be tantamount to giving a burglar in your home a guest pass, fresh towels, breakfast, and a bedroom after he kicked in your back door. What person in their right mind would do that? Once the word reached the street that you were offering guest passes and preferential treatment to burglars, guess what Einstein? Don't be surprised when the entire criminal element in your neighborhood embraces your hospitality.

No. A sane person would toss the bum out and have him arrested. End of story. You don't reward illegal behavior. Especially not when America is living under the constant threat from terrorists. You'd think that Tom

Ridge, who did a fantastic job as the Homeland Security secretary, would have understood the foolishness of such a move.

At least one Republican, Rep. Elton Gallegly, had the guts to stand up and say the king was wearing no clothes. What Gallegly said should have been as obvious to Mr. Bush as a weevil on a Mexican avocado: "Today, national security also dictates that we gain control of our borders. As the September 11 commission and many security professionals have noted, terrorists can easily blend in with the thousands of Mexican nationals who attempt to—and succeed in—crossing our border surreptitiously every day. Our policies are providing cover for our enemies." What's more, he notes, amnesty programs "only encourage more people to cross the border illegally."[2]

Talk about a twofer: Bush effectively outsources millions of jobs to illegal aliens that could have otherwise benefited American workers and, at the same time, encourages more people—some with terrorist ties—to invade our borders to further erode our economic and national security. While there is a modicum of resistance growing in Congress over the guest-worker proposal, I fear President Bush will invoke an executive order to have his way if all else fails.

> **PRESIDENT BUSH IS SO DETERMINED TO HAND MEXICAN WORKERS THE KEYS TO THE COUNTRY HE'S WILLING TO GAMBLE WITH OUR NATIONAL SECURITY.**

Forget what you've been told. This president is not a conservative on the side of trade. A true conservative leader would protect, not permit an alien and economic invasion as Mr. Bush is doing. No wonder he was silent during the debates with John Kerry about outsourcing jobs to Mexican interests.

But there's another facet of this

deception I must note. In December 2004, Bush lobbied Congress to pass his intelligence bill. Buried deep within the fine print, this measure did nothing to stop illegal aliens in many states from obtaining a driver's license![3] How could he do this to us? President Bush is so determined to hand Mexican workers the keys to the country he's willing to gamble with our national security. Of course, that's not the spin he put on the bill. In his radio address, President Bush said, "We must do everything necessary to confront and defeat the terrorist threat, and that includes intelligence reform."[4]

I agree. So, why the doublespeak?

Has he forgotten that the hijackers on September 11 amassed sixty-three driver's licenses? Those IDs were instrumental in the deaths of thousands of American citizens. Haven't we learned our lesson yet? Or has the mental disorder of liberalism so clouded our judgment we no longer see the obvious? Didn't the president read the 9/11 Commission Report? This document specifically pointed out the need for driver's license reform:

> Secure identification should begin in the United States. The federal government should set standards for the issuance of birth certificates and sources of identification, such as driver's licenses. Fraud in identification documents is no longer just a problem of theft. At many entry points to vulnerable facilities, including gates for boarding aircraft, sources of identification are the last opportunity to ensure that people are who they say they are and to check whether they are terrorists.

In my assessment, the IQ of the Intelligence Bill is on the moronic level as long as the bill omits a provision to ban driver's licenses for illegal aliens. Again, in case there is any doubt about the need for reform in this area, the commission's report warned:

> It is elemental to border security to know who is coming into the country. Today more than 9 million people are in the United States outside the legal immigration system. . . . All but one of the 9/11 hijackers acquired some form of U.S. identification document, some by fraud. Acquisition of these forms of identification would have assisted them in boarding commercial flights, renting cars, and other necessary activities.[5]

What's the point of an intelligence overhaul if it stalls out over something as simple as a driver's license ban for illegal aliens? This string of Bush policy positions appears to be a betrayal of our national economic and security interests.

Let's set aside the blindness in the Bush administration for a moment and consider "the traitors" on the left whose sole goal is to make hell for America's most productive "traders."

FISH HAVE FEELINGS, TOO

For years, doctors and dieticians have been telling Americans to eat more fish. The anti-oxidants and other health benefits are abundant. Just as restaurant owners are expanding their menus to include a wider variety of fresh seafood, PETA, People for the Ethical Treatment of Animals, a radical, left-wing, animal-rights pressure group, has launched a national boycott of restaurants who serve fish. Why?

Fish have feelings.

Fish feel pain.

Fish are people, too.

What further evidence do you need that liberalism is a mental disorder? Listen to this lunatic, a spokeschick for The Fish Empathy Project, a new PETA initiative to harass businesses. She explained, "Fish are so misunderstood because they're so far removed from our daily lives. They're such interesting, fascinating individuals, yet they're so incredibly abused."[6]

Stop right there. Fish are what?

Fascinating *individuals?*

What planet is she living on?

This IQ-deficiency case is concerned about the abuse of fish? What about the beheading of civilians at the hands of Islamists? What about the genocide in the Sudan? Not one word from PETA about the torture chambers, the rape rooms, and the iron maidens used to inflict pain on fellow humans during Saddam's rule. No, it's the "cruelty" of the evil fishermen and the feelings of minnows that we're supposed to swallow.

I refuse to take the bait.

At the same time, let me be clear about something. I am an animal lover. And yet I eat meat, I eat fowl, I eat fish. I also believe to attack those who want to protect the environment *across the board* is foolish. Too many Republicans have bought the party line hook, line, and sinker that all environmentalists are wackjobs; that all people who want to keep the bays, the rivers, the oceans, and the skies clean and who want to see the preservation of all

> **TOO MANY REPUBLICANS HAVE BOUGHT THE PARTY LINE HOOK, LINE, AND SINKER THAT ALL ENVIRONMENTALISTS ARE WACKJOBS.**

animal species are all delusional. They're not. Many are the good shepherds of the earth.

Conservatives should be among the most strident protectors of earth and all of its creatures therein. After all, the conservatives are the hunters, the sailors, the boaters and, in that way, are truly in touch with the environment. Can you see Barbara Boxer in her gold lamé heels hiking the Sierras? Or sailing a boat on her own in the bay? I can't. She claims to be an environmentalist and yet she probably doesn't even hike up her own driveway.

Sadly, the conservatives who should be the true environmentalists, who should take the lead to prevent pollution, have become cheerleaders for the most debased element of the industrial machine. That's the heartbreak of it all. The Republicans should own the environmental issue—not just attack those who would preserve nature.

Of course, there *is* an extreme wing of the environmental movement—those who see mankind as somehow *inferior* creatures in the animal kingdom. PETA is the perfect case in point. That hogwash doesn't change the fact that we should never mutilate animals for fun or abuse the environment for profits. Nevertheless, animals are not now—nor will they ever be—people. God created animals for our companionship, our enjoyment, and, yes, for our food. Surprised? You might want to reread Genesis 9:2–3.

That said, PETA's view of fish as *individuals* is fanciful.

A fellow fish-shtick and PETA-spokesmouth carps, "No one would ever put a hook through a dog's or cat's mouth. Once people start to understand that fish, although they come in different packaging, are just as intelligent, they'll stop eating them."[7]

Gee, fish have feelings *and* brains.

But there's more.

While PETA was launching their boycott of seafood restaurants, Jimmy Carter, a fair weather fisherman, snagged himself in the face with his own fishing lure. When news of Carter's painful encounter with a fishhook hit the wires, PETA quickly urged the ex-president to give up fishing. Why? In a letter faxed to Carter's nonprofit Carter Center, PETA appealed to his role as a former Nobel Peace Prize winner, saying, "And we expect that a compassionate world leader like President Carter will agree that [fish] deserve to live in peace."[8]

What's this? If Carter stops fishing, fish worldwide will be so inspired by his example they'll stop devouring each other and live in peace? These guys have gone off the deep end. What PETA fails to comprehend is that the diet of many fish is fellow aquatic travelers. Which begs the question: If fish can eat fish, why can't we?

Benjamin Franklin, who at one point in his life embraced a vegetarian diet, arrived at the same conclusion. Like PETA, he once believed to eat fish was a form of "unprovoked murder" since "none of them had or ever could do us injury that might justify the slaughter." Franklin's view changed in a remarkable way. One day his friends caught and cooked fresh fish which "smelt admirably well." He writes, "I balanced some time between principle and inclination: till I recollected, that when the fish were opened, I saw smaller fish taken out of their stomachs: Then, thought I, if you eat one another, I don't see why we mayn't eat you."[9]

You see, in PETA's perfect world, we'd all be eating wild grass clippings and tofu chowder while Red Lobster snaps shut, Long John Silver walks the plank, and tuna fish is banned from school lunches. In their perfect world, any business caught selling fish would be fined and forced to attend a fish *eeeempathy* class. This is a classic case of *Animal Farm* with a twist: Two fins good; two legs bad.

> THIS IS A CLASSIC CASE OF ANIMAL FARM WITH A TWIST: TWO FINS GOOD; TWO LEGS BAD.

Forget that. I refuse to be distracted from genuine human suffering, the mass graves, the throat-cutters, and the suicide bombers for misguided, do-gooder fish tales about the unethical treatment of aquatic creatures. Year after year, innocent Jewish children are targeted in Israel and the West Bank while all this left-wing front group cares about is the Outer Banks.

Tell me that such ignorance and liberal indoctrination is not a mental disorder.

Look, I can't help it if the PETA staff have watched *Finding Nemo* and *Free Willy* until their minds have become as polluted as Lake Michigan. But I can do my part to expose these morally twisted frauds. They'd rather throw restaurant owners out of business and toss the fishermen overboard than disturb the emotional welfare of a sardine.

Maybe somebody should explain to PETA that "Charley the Tuna" wasn't a real "individual."

CROSS-DRESSED FOR SUCCESS

Here's another perfect example of how the psychopathic liberals are determined to send this great nation down the road to ruin through draconian regulations, which, at the risk of being redundant, is a byproduct of their mental disorder. On April 21, 2003, the Demoncat-controlled California Assembly passed AB 196, a bill authorizing fines up to $150,000 against any business owner (including churches, schools, and nonprofit organizations like the Boy Scouts) who refuses to employ transgender or cross-dressing applicants.

Can you believe this?

The state senate, in turn, went along with this lunacy, quickly passing the initiative after a mere forty-five minutes of debate. Not surprisingly, all of the "yes" votes came from the Democrats. The bill also expanded the definition of "gender" in the Fair Employment and Housing Act to include "identity, appearance, or behavior, whether or not that identity, appearance, or behavior is different from that traditionally associated with the victim's sex at birth."

Victim?

Imagine what would happen if a transvestite applied for work at Ethel's Bible Bookstore. Ethel may be seventy-five years old, but she's not blind. She knows her clientele would shop elsewhere if a cross-dresser with a nose ring worked the cash register. If Ethel were to turn down the she-male, under this law she could be fined $150,000 by the Department of Fair Employment and Housing. No doubt she'd be forced into bankruptcy, and I wouldn't be surprised if she were carted off to a *sensitiiiivity* camp as they chained the doors behind her.

As I said at the outset, the anti-capitalist, pro-socialist liberals seek to intimidate, regulate, tax, and sue businesses into compliance with their worldview. That's why Gray Davis, then-governor of California, signed the measure into law, which took effect January 1, 2004. Due to the mental disease of liberalism and his signature on the measure, California became the fourth state to create such a nightmare for businesses. Michigan, New Mexico, and Rhode Island have similar provisions.

This means that in California, the fruit bowl of liberal madness, if Johnny who wants to be Jenny applies for a job, and if I don't hire him/her/it or whatever, I can be sued and fined for discrimination. Hold on.

Why can't I, as a business owner, make decisions that will enhance, not harm, my profit potential?

Why should I be required to hire someone who has the potential of repelling customers?

Isn't it a fundamental right for a business owner to have an appearance standard or dress code?

And since when did sexual reassignment become a civil rights issue? Where is that in the Constitution?

> SOMEHOW I CAN'T PICTURE MARTIN LUTHER KING JR. MARCHING IN MAKEUP AND A MINISKIRT TO HOLD A VIGIL AT THE STATE CAPITAL FOR THE RIGHTS OF DRAG QUEENS.

Somehow I can't picture Martin Luther King Jr. marching in makeup and a miniskirt to hold a vigil at the state capital for the rights of drag queens.

Mark my words. The day will come when some half-wit legislator will propose a bill to apply affirmative action statues to transgender persons. Why? It's a fact that transgender-benders in San Fransicko experience a 70 percent unemployment rate.[10] In the interest of *fairrrrrness,* the libs will argue that mom and pop stores, churches, and schools should be required to have at least one transgender person as an employee.

GLOBALISTS PAINT US RED

Such meddling with private business practices is not the exception. It's become the rule. The American workplace has been infected by a witch's brew of mandates concocted by the left-leaning courts, the insatiable legislators, and the bureaucratic lackeys. From "harassment" and age discrimination laws, to the accommodation of handicapped persons, civil unions, and family leave, employers have become liable for a vast menu of litigation options in this sue-happy culture.

Today's employer must constantly look over his shoulder for the disgruntled employee who might just sue for "wrongful termination" when they've been fired for downloading porn on a company computer on company time. Or maybe sue for causing emotional *distreeess* by harsh supervision, when all you did was ask them to report to work on time.

Globalists love to burden business. They complain about job losses out of one side of their face (as John Kerry did during the campaign of 2004) while slandering the job makers with the other. Heavy-handed regulation and a web of red tape tie up money that could go to invest in jobs—instead, these funds must be spent to comply with a growing mountain of rules.

You see, the globalists hit you from several different directions. They can get what they want from you by taxing you for some redistribution of wealth scheme. Or they can get what they want by making you pay for it yourself. That's what regulations are all about. They're the rules the lawmakers who never worked a day in a hotdog stand impose on businesses that cost time and money to comply with. And these rules are nothing more than an indirect tax that stifles the economy.

The Washington, D.C.-based Cato Institute issues a yearly report called "Ten Thousand Commandments" that shows the impact of these rules. In fact, there are so many regulations that the individual ones aren't really counted. They just count the total pages in the *Federal Register,* which is the daily dumping ground for all these rules. In 2003, the *Federal Register* had 71,269 pages.[11]

We all know that small business is the lifeblood of the economy. Whether it's a local pizza shop, dental firm, or hair salon, these small businesses represent more than 99.7 percent of all U.S. employers. According to the most recent figures, during the year 1999–2000 small businesses created three-fourths of the new jobs in America. But instead of encouraging those who are pursuing the American dream of self-employment, the government conjures up new rules to regulate your business. Why?

Because they think the sheeple are too stupid to know what they're doing.

Who has time to run a business when there are so many restrictions to comply with? No wonder half of the small businesses started today will last only four years.[12]

It's not hard to see how there could be

> **YOU'VE GOT THE EEOC, THE FDA, THE SEC, THE FCC, THE USDA, THE CPSC, THE DOE, THE NHTSA, THE EPA—AND THAT'S JUST FOR STARTERS.**

so many regulations. You've got the EEOC, the FDA, the SEC, the FCC, the USDA, the CPSC, the DOE, the NHTSA, the EPA—and that's just for starters. How does this impact you and me? The average citizen pays about $6,500 in taxes, but the average household gets socked for an additional $8,000 to cover hidden regulatory costs.[13]

"Ten Thousand Commandments" shows the cost of all this regulation runs about $869 billion a year. Environmental regulations are about $203 billion of that number; workplace rule compliance is $85 billion; economic costs like price controls contribute $448 billion; and complying with the tax code adds an additional $133 billion. That's not the amount of the taxes, mind you. That's the amount it costs *on top of the taxes* just to "properly" pay the taxes.[14]

These costs hit the little guy the hardest.

Small businesses, those with fewer than twenty employees, get hammered. To comply with all these regulations, it costs small businesses almost $7,000 per employee—that's in addition to the cost of the employee's salary and payroll taxes.[15] It's easy to see why businesses are struggling and have a hard time hiring new people, not to mention trying to avoid laying people off. The government chokes employers by burying them in rules.

And what if an employer slips up?

When a company overlooks, ignores, or violates even a comma of the employment law, in swoop the vultures.

In some cases, employers get in trouble if they don't test for drugs; on the other hand, they get sued if an employee feels discriminated against if they do. Employers can be sued for enforcing "English Only" rules in the workplace, but they can also be sued if they don't. They can get sued if they give a bad employee reference, but they can also get sued if they fail to inform a prospective new employer that the employee was a drunk. They can get sued for hiring family members, which could be unfair to unrelated minorities, and sued if they ban nepotism, which could be unfair to married couples who want to work.[16]

You're sued if you do and sued if you don't.

Are you starting to get the picture?

THE RULE OF LAWYERS

In my view, anyone who disguises himself as a compassionate person just to line his own pockets ought to be put in a stockade in the public square. Which is why I must turn the Savage microscope on the tort racket perfected by the bloodsucking trial lawyers.

Did you know that in 2001 the trial lawyers as an "industry" grossed *50 percent more revenue* than Microsoft? Did you know these RDDB trial lawyers also successfully sued so many businesses that their combined earnings eclipsed Coca-Cola's revenues by $22 billion?

You might want to read that one again.

This out-of-control, unregulated industry bilks $200 *billion* each year from American businesses by goring them with exorbitant judgments.[17] From 1975 to 2001, tort system costs totaled more than $2.8 trillion! That doesn't include the outrageous tobacco settlement, or most "contract and shareholder litigation costs, most punitive damages costs, or any indirect costs such as defensive medicine or reduced innovation or investment."[18] And, when you consider that about 20

> THIS OUT-OF-CONTROL, UNREGULATED INDUSTRY BILKS $200 BILLION EACH YEAR FROM AMERICAN BUSINESSES BY GORING THEM WITH EXORBITANT JUDGMENTS.

percent of these tort costs go directly to the plaintiffs' attorneys, you begin to see why trial lawyers flock to class action and mass tort suits like maggots on road kill.

TRIAL LAWYERS FLOCK TO CLASS ACTION AND MASS TORT SUITS LIKE MAGGOTS ON ROAD KILL.

Here's how their scam works.

The legal leeches start by stuffing wads of cash into the coffers of politicians to remain unregulated. In Jimmy Hoffa's day these would be called payoffs. With 86 percent of their political contributions going to Democrat candidates, you can guess where the sympathies of the trial lawyers lie. In 2001–2002 (which are the latest available figures), the Association of Trial Lawyers of America was the Democrats' leading Political Action Committee donor, surpassing even the labor unions.

Once the politicians are in their back pocket, they use aggressive marketing techniques to acquire new plaintiffs—not because they care about actual harm done to people. No. They just need these sheeple as pawns toward greater profits. They comb the Internet and flood their target markets with newspaper, TV, radio, and billboard ads, ever in search of fresh meat for their predatory litigation. That's why metro-buses are wallpapered with those placards: *"Injured on the job? Call for our FREE class-action evaluation. You pay nothing until we win your case!"*

Armed with a new batch of real or imagined victims, they target specific deep-pocketed industries (tobacco, beef, asbestos, doctors, insurers, and pharmaceuticals). Then, in order to look as innocent as your grandmother in a Sunday dress, they employ creative PR campaigns and align themselves with consumer "advocacy groups" so you think they're on the side of the victims against the "ruthless doctors," "big business," or the "greedy" drug companies.

Take, for example, the avalanche of asbestos-related lawsuits—a favorite trial lawyer cash cow that squeezed $54 *billion* from corporations to date. This is the longest-running mass tort scam in our history. To date, sixty-seven companies have been forced into bankruptcy, including Owens Corning Fiberglass, Bethlehem Steel, Pittsburgh Corning, USG Corporation, Johns-Manville, and W.R. Grace. Talk about losing jobs. Tens of thousands of families are out of work because of the predatory litigation by trial lawyers. Many of the sixty-seven businesses never even manufactured or sold asbestos products or services. That little detail didn't stop the Briefcase Mafia from suing them out of business.

According to a recent report, companies bankrupted by asbestos have "slashed an estimated 60,000 jobs, failed to create 128,000 new jobs, and forgone an estimated $10 billion in investments."[19]

You see, the trial lawyers have used junk science and fear tactics to wring confiscatory awards from clueless juries. We all know asbestos can cause cancer. If and when it does, some form of compensation is in order. However, just 7 percent of the parties filing these asbestos claims contracted lung or other cancers! Put another way, over 90 percent of the "injured" persons didn't exhibit the cancer-related illness attributed to asbestos exposure.

What the Briefcase Mafia is doing is nothing short of organized extortion, without the gun. At the current pace these bogus claims are being filed, the cost of the "tort tax" on our businesses over the next ten years will be "over $4.8 trillion—almost *triple* the size of the 2001 and 2003 Bush tax cuts *combined*."[20]

Billion, trillion, schmillion—what's it to you? As long as you're getting your cable porn, food stamps, and medical marijuana, none of this matters to you, does it? It should. Staggering sums of money are being extracted from the traders by the traitors.

> EVERY TIME SOME LOSER IS HANDED A MULTIMILLION-DOLLAR AWARD FOR SPILLING HOT MCDONALD'S COFFEE ON THEIR LAP, THE PRICE OF AN EGG MCMUFFIN GOES UP.

Every time some loser is handed a multimillion-dollar award for spilling hot McDonald's coffee on their lap, the price of an Egg McMuffin goes up.

Every time a hospital is sued for malpractice because a patient intentionally jumps from a parking garage to commit suicide yet lives and collects $9 million, which, in turn, raises your cost of health care, thank a trial lawyer.[21]

When Seong Sil Kim, a New York nut, patiently lies in front of a train to commit suicide, but lives after the train hits her hand and is awarded $9.9 million in damages causing your fares to go up and service to go down, thank a trial lawyer.[22] On the other hand, I imagine we should count our blessings. Seong Kim was originally awarded $14.1 million. But the judge, who should have tossed the case out in the first place, reduced the reward to $9.9 million after determining that Kim shared a 30 percent portion of the blame for the incident.

In the medical field, because of rising medical-malpractice rates due to these gangsters with law degrees, doctors resort to practicing "defensive medicine"—medical testing requested just to avoid legal liability. Which is why 80 percent of doctors order unneeded tests while 74 percent refer patients to other specialists so they don't get sued.[23]

Can there be any question that the legal gangs have made a mockery of our legal system and are stifling businesses? How about this evidence that the inmates are running the system:

A twenty-seven-year-old male prostitute with "gender identity issues" attempted to hang himself in his jail cell, but botched the effort resulting in brain damage. He sued the city of Philadelphia for $50 million. On what grounds? His lawyers argued that their client should have been placed in a suicide-watch cell, not a conventional police cell. Rather than expend resources to defend itself, the city decided to settle the lawsuit for $3.5 million.[24]

If you think that's bad, read on.

Vice president hopeful John Edwards, a rapacious trial lawyer, actually pretended to channel the words of a yet-to-be born, breeched baby girl. During his final arguments in one case, Edwards told the jury, "She said at 3, 'I'm fine.' She said at 4, 'I'm having a little trouble, but I'm OK.' Five, she said, 'I'm having problems.' At 5:30, she said, 'I need out.'" Edwards went on to say, "And I have to tell you right now—I didn't plan to talk about this—right now I feel her. I feel her presence. She's inside me, and she's talking to you."[25] This little vaudeville performance was supposed to demonstrate that the doctor's lack of an immediate Caesarean section caused the baby to have brain damage.

The jury bought his act and awarded the plaintiff a $6.5 million verdict.

Thank God this snake oil salesman didn't become the vice president.

Elsewhere, Ted Smith, executive director of the Florida Auto Dealers Associations, reports there are a dozen lawyers who have carved out a nice living *just suing car dealerships*. Smith says, "The Florida litigation environment for dealers is an evolving nightmare. It is a norm to see an attorney bring a case for damages of $10,000 and a court award of $200,000 in attorneys' fees."[26]

And you wonder why car prices are so high.

Likewise, trial lawyers in California are driving away with huge profits, having sued 1,200 car dealerships over "technical violations" made "in newspaper advertisements (i.e. wrong font size of the print or using the common acronym 'A.P.R.' instead of spelling out 'Annual Percentage

Rate'). The dealers settled for about $10,000 each." Guess what? There wasn't one customer or business asking the lawyers to file a complaint over the fine print. The trial lawyers did it on their own and pocketed $10 million.

Of course, $10 million is chump change when compared to the $4.9 billion—you read that right, *billion*—award doled out to *six people*. Why? A drunk driver slammed into the rear of Patricia Anderson's 1979 Chevy Malibu as she waited at a red light. According to the lawyers for GM, the drunk was speeding at seventy miles per hour. That impact was "the equivalent of dropping the car from top of a sixteen-story building."[27] All six people in Patricia's car lived—which is a real testament to the design of that Malibu.

The trial lawyers didn't see it that way.

When Patricia's gas tank caught fire due to the crash, she and the others suffered severe burns. With the scent of big corporate dollars lingering in the air, the lawyers representing the passengers claimed GM's gas tank placement was a "faulty design" and thus, responsible for the burns. Forget about the fact that over the twenty years prior, the National Highway Traffic Safety Administration never once deemed the Malibu's gas tank placement to be a hazard. On July 9, 1999, a Los Angeles jury sided with Patricia and friends, and ordered General Motors to pay a record $4.9 billion—a number they plucked out of thin air.

I'd say a little perspective is in order: $4.9 billion is a big number. But how big was it? How about the fact that it eclipsed the total sales from all Subway restaurants in the United States in 1999! If there's any justice to be found in this runaway judgment, the award was later reduced to $1.2 billion.[28]

According to the Manhattan Institute, "the lawsuit industry even has its own venture capitalists—investors who back firms filing enormous, speculative class-action suits with the hope that there will be rich rewards some-where down the road—and its own secondary financial market, where shares in future legal fees are bought and sold."[29] Lawsuits over mold, for instance, have created the new "black gold rush." Again, even though the science doesn't support the claims, there's plenty of fear-mongering to go around about the dangers of mold lurking in your basement. The trial lawyers are seeing big dollar signs attached to that new frontier.

Just ask Ed McMahon, the late Johnny Carson's former sidekick on the *Tonight Show,* who was awarded $7.2 million after claiming that the mold in his house killed his dog.[30] Look, I'm a dog owner. I'm sorry for McMahon's loss. But how can a pet be valued at $7 million?

Is it any wonder manufacturers of various products now feel that they must spell out the obvious in order to avoid being slapped with a massive lawsuit? This handful of examples would be funny if they didn't present such a clear picture of how we've lost our minds: An iron manufacturer cautions, *"Never iron clothes while they're being worn."* A notice on a toilet at a sports facility in Ann Arbor, Michigan, warned: *"Recycled flush water unsafe for drinking."* Or the electric wood router used by carpenters which offered this caveat, *"This product not intended for use as a dental drill."* And the warning on a bottle of sleeping pills which exclaimed, *"May cause drowsiness."*

I realize this may seem somewhat removed from where you live. Maybe you just can't connect the dots. Consider this. A recent study shows U.S. tort costs in 2002 were $223 billion—that's 2.23 percent of the gross domestic product thrown away on higher prices, higher insurance premiums, lower standard of

> IN REAL DOLLARS, IT'S LIKE LAWYERS DEDUCTING MORE THAN $800 OFF THE TOP OF YOUR YEARLY SALARY!

living, etc. In real dollars, it's like lawyers deducting more than $800 off the top of *your* yearly salary.[31]

When money is sucked out of the economy on frivolous lawyers fees, businesses are prevented from investing in new hires, stronger benefits for workers, or otherwise expanding their market. The only people benefiting are the Briefcase Mafia.

A WALK TO REMEMBER

As you know, Michael Savage is a man of the streets and a man of the people. I don't just sit in a radio studio surfing the Internet for interesting topics. I walk among the people. One day recently I had my lunch and then took a long walk around San Francisco. One of my favorite places to stop is a little-known urban park called the TransAmerica Redwood Park.

The TransAmerica Tower is a gorgeous building in downtown San Francisco that the liberal psychos tried to stop when it was originally being designed. They said it didn't fit into the city. These claptrap antiquarians wanted dilapidated firetraps forever. Anyway, over their protests, a gorgeous tower unlike any other building was built, embellished with a little park next to it.

In Redwood Park several incredibly beautiful sculptures are on display. One is so lyrical—it's called *Frog Pond* by Richard Clopton. It's a fairly large pond that splashes a lot of water in the middle of the city with bronze frogs leaping and jumping on lily pads.

Another nearby sculpture is a cluster of six happy, skipping children in ragamuffin outfits, poised as though they're jumping at you. They're called *Puddle Jumpers* by Glenna Goodacre. Gorgeous.

As I stood there drinking my coffee, I started to say to myself, "Do you realize that *Frog Pond* and the *Puddle Jumpers* would not be approved by the mean-spirited brown shirts running San Francisco's art world today?" Do you realize what they would force you to put there?

Probably two men kissing on a wedding cake.

Then another thought hit me.

We need to dream. We need to create. We, as the producers and workers, need to believe that the world we envision in our heads can become real if we want it to. Because without dreams, we lose the battle for the future of America before it begins. Without dreams, we are nothing. We are no better than the cavemen in Krapistan who contribute nothing to the betterment of the world.

As I finished lunch, my mind wandered back to my father and my childhood. My father has been dead some thirty years, God rest his soul. In spite of all of my travels and education, that man taught me more about the value of money, hard work, personal achievement, and pursuing dreams than anyone.

My father didn't want to give me a penny. As an immigrant, he didn't have a penny to give. He really didn't make a lot of money. Now, don't get me wrong. We had a house, the meals, the clothes, and I went to a city college. I didn't suffer. But what he did give me was priceless.

He used to lecture me in the living room—a lot. He'd give these tirades walking back and forth in an undershirt. Which is where I got it from. You could say my father was a born talk-show host without a microphone. So, he'd get up in the living room and read about some rich snot-nose who did something horrendous and he'd say, "You see what inherited wealth does? If I had money, I wouldn't leave a nickel to my children."

I'm sitting there like a dummy, listening. No one else in the room. He'd say, "I'd give it to the ASPCA." That's the humane society. In his view, the dogs should get it. They needed it. Not children. Why? Children of the rich became spoiled junkies and perverts. In his own way, my father was giving me a heads-up that to get ahead, I needed to work, to apply myself, to take whatever talents God gave me and pursue my dreams. Not steal money, as a trial lawyer!

That's why as imperfect as capitalism is, the practice of free enterprise is the best system the world has ever seen. And that's also why I detest the efforts of the traitors to derail the dreams of the traders.

THE SAVAGE SOLUTION

Too many politicians have come to regard the state and all affairs of the state as their private property. State political committees of both parties and state party bosses form a sort of grand private club of American politics which has its own signs and passwords. It is a creed of this class that the public business is theirs and theirs alone to manipulate as they see fit.

So, on one hand, we could turn over our paychecks to the government and let them run the whole show. Of course, that would be socialism. No, I say we must stop the traitors. How?

First, stop outsourcing our industries. As I warned my radio audience back in 1994, when Nazism arrived in America, it wouldn't necessarily announce itself. When I said history is going to repeat itself but in a different form, many thought I was an extremist. But I was right. Today the socio-fascists are marching with another symbol on its arm: the badge of *compaaaaassion*.

> LET'S CUT THE CRAP. WHEN IT COMES TO STIMULATING BUSINESS, GEORGE W. BUSH MUST START LEADING THIS COUNTRY.

Let's cut the crap. When it comes to stimulating business, George W. Bush must start leading *this* country. I say take on the left, Mr. Bush. Reject their call to globalize our economy. Refuse the push to outsource work. India, China, and Mexico are not the fifty-first, fifty-second, and fifty-third states. Get out there in the trenches with us and fight to defend the little guy who's just trying to make a buck. Stop handing our future to the cheats and sneaks. Show some compassion to the family farms and the producers in your *own* country.

That's the message we must drive home not only to the president, but also to our evidently clueless elected representatives in Congress.

Second, cut corporate taxation. Millions of dollars are tied up in offshore businesses—more than $600 million, according to the Congressional Research Service. These funds are not invested in American domestic employment because of the high corporate tax rates.

As Lawrence J. McQuillan of the Pacific Research Institute explains, to bring some of that money home the Dems floated a plan that would give corporations a one-year break on the money they make through their offshore subsidiaries; instead of paying the full 35 percent corporate tax, they'd pay just 10 percent on any money they reinvested in the American side of their businesses. After the one-year break, however, foreign subsidiaries would pay 33.25 percent. What—do these people have cream cheese for brains? If this plan went forward, after the one-year break companies would have an incentive to *leave* the U.S. because of the tax savings!

Given what we know about taxes dragging the economy, we ought to cut corporate taxes to zero. That would not only make America competitive, quell outsourcing, and bring home jobs, it would lead to massive insourcing—other nations bringing their jobs here. Granted, a dip in the U.S. Treasury would follow the elimination of corporate taxation, but the increased creation of jobs with the related taxable income should more than offset this. Reagan proved that the economy does best when people have control over their own money. The same principle applies to corporations.

Third, unravel the red tape. Business regulations are choking America.

Since it's the overall cost of business—not just cheap labor or taxes—that sends companies overseas, this is one area that needs drastic reshaping. Not only will this enable us to be more competitive on the global scale, it will help us do more to grow the economy at home. Less regulation means more economic freedom, and more economic freedom means more business and jobs.

LAWYERS ARE LIKE RED WINE. EVERYTHING IN MODERATION. TODAY WE HAVE FAR TOO MANY LAWYERS, AND WE'RE SUFFERING FROM CIRRHOSIS OF THE ECONOMY.

Fourth, pass tort reform now. Lawyers are important to a society of laws. But lawyers are like red wine. Everything in moderation. Today we have far too many lawyers, and we're suffering from cirrhosis of the economy.

To fix this plague, there must be strict caps placed on the highly subjective pain-and-suffering damage awards; getting hefty awards for punitive damages must be made more difficult; and a new standard must be set governing joint liability laws. These and other provisions are addressed in The Class Action Fairness Act of 2003, a bill introduced into the Senate and the House. The measure stalled in both bodies, but the issue is far from dead.

With fifty-five Republicans in the Senate, and a number of pro-tort reform Democrat allies, Mr. Bush, who brought significant tort reform to Texas, has been handed a golden opportunity to bring much needed tort relief to rest of the country.

Before leaving this subject, there's one more thing that must be said about too many in both parties. If the people who landed at Plymouth Rock were only out for themselves, this nation never would have been founded; indeed, our achievements and contributions to world history would never have materialized.

We must keep up the drumbeat of fire against these swindlers. We must continue to assert the rights of *We the People* to create jobs and wealth in spite of the efforts to stifle the freedom to build and earn by the sweat of our brows.

FIVE

ARAFAT, CLINTON, KINSEY: SYMPATHY FOR THE DEVIL

The American media has gone to the dark side. Intoxicated with their power, these empty souls routinely put a corkscrew to world events, twisting the news to fit their leftist view of history. The death of Yasser Arafat in November of 2004 best typifies their insanity. The way the media covered his crossing the river Styx, you'd think Arafat was Abe Lincoln in a turban.

How quickly the media elite suffered willful mass amnesia.

Arafat was a monster. This walking obscenity invented airline hijacking, hostage taking, school massacres, and suicide bombings. He kept the Palestinians in a prison of moral, spiritual, and economic poverty. He embezzled their money and, during his final years, skimmed more than $2 million a month to line his pockets.[1]

> ARAFAT WAS A MONSTER. THIS WALKING OBSCENITY INVENTED AIRLINE HIJACKING, HOSTAGE TAKING, SCHOOL MASSACRES, AND SUICIDE BOMBINGS. HE KEPT THE PALESTINIANS IN A PRISON OF MORAL, SPIRITUAL, AND ECONOMIC POVERTY.

And let's not forget he turned an entire generation of children into psychopaths.

But you'd never know these facts, not if you picked up a mainstream paper or watched the news in the wake of his death. No, the media glorified him and they adored him; they admired him as a "freedom fighter" in a just cause against the oppression of the Israelis.

Take the *Old York Times*. Pinchy's paper called Arafat an "enigmatic statesman," and had the audacity to reduce Arafat's acts of terrorism to nothing more than "public relations"[2] stunts. After gushing over Arafat's contribution to the Palestinians, the *Times* took its magic wand and—*presto!*—changed his hijackings to "air piracy" and his acts of mass murder to "innovative forms of mayhem staged for maximum propaganda value."[3]

Innovative?

If Pinchy means that this thug was the forerunner of Osama bin Laden then, yes, he'd be right. In which case the *Times* should have dubbed him: Arafat, the Godfather of al-Qaida. I'm sure the Jewish mothers who begged for the lives of their children massacred while trapped on a school bus will appreciate knowing Arafat's attacks were "innovative."

USA Today was equally complicit. In its report, just four words hinted at his long history of terrorism. It reported that Arafat was "revered as the champion of Palestinian statehood" and—here's the razor-thin reference to his atrocities—was "reviled as a terrorist."[4]

That's it? Forty years of state-sponsored terrorism and this arch-terrorist gets a footnote?

Could you imagine living in 1945, picking up the paper, and reading, "A German leader, Adolf Hitler, dies at 67, a controverrrsial figure who was reviled and revered." What journalist would have written such a thing in those days? If Hitler lived today, I'm confident the leftist media machine would completely gloss over his slaughtering of six million Jews. No question. In fact, we saw that with Saddam Hussein, that Hitler in a headscarf, who gassed his own people, dumping their bodies in open pits.

As I scanned the media for an accurate portrayal of Arafat's trail of blood, I visited MSNBC's Web site where I found a photo essay of his life. Guess what? It featured one heroic pose after another. I started checking my eyes, you know, had I missed something? Not one photo of his countless acts of terrorism.

Not one! You'd think this mass murderer was George Washington reincarnate.

How could this be? Arafat the Barbarian was to the right of Attila the Hun. That should have been how he was depicted. Instead, his Hitleresque view of the Jews was completely whitewashed from all news reports by ABC, CBS, and NBC. None of these left-wing newsrooms could bring itself to report the truth, not even Fox. Worse, with help from clueless world leaders, they did the complete opposite by venerating the killer.

With the United Nations' blue and white flag flying at half-mast, Coffee Cup Annan blathered that Arafat the Terrorist "expressed and symbolized in his person the national aspirations of the Palestinian people."[5] Not to be upstaged, Jacques Chirac called the homicidal Arafat a "man of courage and conviction,"[6] while Gerhard Schroeder, the socialist weasel, said, "it was not granted to Yasser Arafat to complete his life's work."[7]

What work? The annihilation of Israel?

This is more than a disgrace; it's an outrage!

If these news agencies had a shred of journalistic integrity, instead of parroting praises they would have pictured a family gunned down by a Palestine Liberation Organization (PLO) sniper hiding behind a rock at the side of the road. They would have pictured planes shot out of the sky, pictured a school bus blown up by the PLO, or pictured the mutilated bodies blown up by Arafat's psychos in a crowded Israeli pizzeria.

And so I must ask, why didn't the press tell the truth? It certainly can't be for a lack of knowledge. I'm just one man. I don't have a news department to do my research. And yet I can find out the truth about this terrorist in two seconds on the Web.

At the top of Arafat's résumé is the term "Arch Terrorist." We know this. How can the newsrooms across America not know that he was a monster? This would be like forgetting that Babe Ruth played baseball. Does the PLO have their bloodied fingers in the back pockets of the American media? Or, does our leftist-run media have an axe to grind with Israel?

I'll let you be the judge.

Yasser Arafat brought terrorism to our age, and the truth must be told. The legacy of this madman must be correctly recorded for posterity, which I gladly do. Let's be clear: Arafat was not the Winston Churchill of the Middle East, as Peter Jennings and Katie "Koran" Couric would have you believe. Nor was he, as Jimmy Carter—that failure of a president—said, "a very moderate person"[8] just trying to pursue a homeland and the betterment of his people. Wrong. There was nothing moderate about the man.

The real legacy of Arafat runs crimson red. But you don't know that because you've been fed a fictional account by the media. That's why I'm going to go into some detail to show you the truth about this monster. What follows is a map to hell paved with blood shed by Mohammed Yasser Abdel-Ra'ouf Qudwa Al-Hussaeini—our man Arafat.

FROM PLAYPEN TO PLAYGROUND: JIHAD JANIE

There are some things in life that the human mind cannot fathom. Near the top of that list would be the act of breeding babies to be suicide bombers. And yet, Yasser Arafat and the PLO spent years perfecting the process of indoctrinating Jew-hatred in the minds of children through state-sponsored TV, in textbooks for preteens, and at teen summer camping programs.

No wonder the hatred runs deep.

Take, for example, *The Children's Club,* a prime-time television favorite that played in homes throughout Palestine. In many ways it's no different than Sesame Street—you know, the puppets, the props, the dancing, the kids sitting in a circle singing—but with a deadly twist. Granted, there wasn't an exploding Khalid the Muppet character with a strap-on explosives belt. They didn't need one. Instead, fresh-faced kids, some appearing to be no more than five years old, sang songs celebrating the day when they'd spill their blood as a suicide bomber.

In the February 13, 1998, episode, the camera zoomed in to frame the face of one tot. Although singing somewhat off-key, her zeal was unmistakable: "Oh my sister, sing constantly about my life as a suicide warrior. Each and every part of your soil I have drenched with all my blood, and we shall march as warriors of jihad."

It's out with Cookie Monster, in with Jihad Janie.

IT'S OUT WITH COOKIE MONSTER, IN WITH JIHAD JANIE.

With young girls swaying to the music and little boys raising their arms skyward, the following sound bites from this PLO kid's TV show were taken straight from the mouth of babes— literally no more than ten years old. What did these Palestinian youths want to be when they grow up? As Mickey Mouse danced across the TV screen, the kids stared into the camera and boasted before an audience of impressionable young minds:

- February 6, 1998: "When I wander into the entrance of Jerusalem, I'll turn into a suicide warrior, in battledress."

- March 21, 1998: "Ask from us blood, we will drench you. Ask from us our soul, we will give it to you."

- May 22, 1998: "I shall take my soul in my hand and throw it into the abyss of death. On your life I foresee my death. But I march quickly towards my death. Am I afraid? For me life has little value. Because I am returning to my Lord, and my people will know I am a hero."

- July 2, 1998: "Occupier, your day is near, then we will settle our account. We will settle our claims with stones and bullets."

This was the sort of deranged TV programming produced by the Palestinian Authority five years after Yasser Arafat shook hands with President Bill Clinton and Yitzchak Rabin at the White House. Remember that one? The meeting was supposed to mark a new day in the relationship between the PLO and Israel. But in reality that headscarfed Trojan horse smiled for the cameras with his fingers crossed behind his back.

Why am I not surprised that Arafat conveniently ignored the details of the Oslo II agreement and produced his reprehensible terror tots TV show? Article XXII specifically charges the Palestine Authority and Israel to "seek to foster mutual understanding and tolerance and shall accordingly abstain from incitement, including hostile propaganda, against each other." Asking Arafat to abide by that guideline would have been like asking Hitler to close the death camps. Yet, Clinton believed the monster!

That's not all. Are you sitting down?

This terror primer for tots was funded in part by your tax dollars! You heard me. During the Clinton era, the Voice of Palestine, which produced *The Children's Club,* received dollars from U.S. Aid for International Development (USAID), an agency that reports to the White House.[9] To be specific, make that "about $500,000 in equipment and training," so says Radwan Abu Ayash, the chairman of Palestinian Broadcasting

Corporation (PBC) television.[10]

Moving beyond the playpen crowd, preteens are taught political violence in their textbooks. This, from a fifth-grade Arabic language text: "Remember: the final and inevitable result will be the victory of the Muslims over the Jews . . . the Nation will recruit its forces and there will be a jihad and our country will be freed."[11]

And this from an eighth-grade reader and literary text: "My brothers! The oppressors have overstepped the boundary, therefore jihad and sacrifice are a duty . . . let us gather for war with red blood and blazing fire . . . Oh, Palestine, the youth will redeem your land."[12]

Tell me those students aren't being brainwashed into a psychopathic death cult.

The same teens steeped in songs of hatred for the Jews since they could hold a rattle can attend a summer camp hosted by the Palestinian Authority. There, war tactics and the military training of children is the name of the game. Leave it to the religion of peace to hold a camp with the theme, "Fifty years of occupation: We will not forget and we will not forgive."[13]

Don't for one second believe the lie from Coffee Cup Annan that Arafat wanted a peaceful coexistence between Israel and the future Palestinian state. He's lying. Yasser Arafat never accepted the idea of coexistence or a two-state solution. He always believed in just one solution, which was the same solution as what Hitler had in store: The Final Solution.

Need more proof?

Yasser Arafat, speaking on the Palestinian Authority TV network January 15, 2002, said, "This child, who is grasping the stone, facing the tank: Is it not the greatest message to the world when that hero becomes a martyr? We are proud of them."[14] And, on May 16, 2004, six months before his death, Arafat gave a speech to the Palestinians in which he said, "Find whatever strength you have to terrorize your enemy."[15]

Just what we'd expect from a Nobel Peace Prize winner.

But, you might ask, Arafat signed the Oslo Accords in 1993, didn't he? Forget about it. That was nothing more than a publicity stunt. The Oslo Accords, incidentally, were constructed by the Clintonistas who almost destroyed the state of Israel in their quest to win a Nobel Peace Prize. The fact of the matter is that the Oslo Accords were nothing more than a blueprint for the death of the Jewish people and for the state of Israel.

> **ARAFAT NEVER WANTED PEACE. HE WANTED A PIECE OF FLESH. THE FLESH OF DEAD JEWS.**

Bill Clinton, if not the architect, was most certainly the messenger; and Madeleine Halfbright was nothing less than a yenta who ran along with it screaming, "Oslo! Oslo! Oslo!" like it was the Holy Grail when the fact of the matter is they almost gave away all of Israel for a little bit of phony peace.

Arafat never wanted peace. He wanted a piece of flesh.

The flesh of dead Jews.

BLAST FROM THE PAST

On October 7, 1985, Leon and Marilyn Klinghoffer boarded the *Achille Lauro,* an Italian luxury liner, to celebrate their thirty-sixth anniversary. Both were U.S. citizens, Jewish, and lived in New York. At sixty-nine, Leon was wheelchair-bound, having suffered a series of strokes. I'm sure he envisioned a relaxing cruise in the Mediterranean. That dream turned to a nightmare when Mohammed Abu Abbas and three PLO terrorists were accidentally caught cleaning their weapons by a cabin steward.

Abbas, armed with guns, grenades, and ammo, had planned to sneak into Israel to carry out a terrorist attack. With his cover blown, Abbas hijacked the 400-passenger ship and demanded the release of fifty

Palestinian prisoners held by the Israeli government. Egyptian President Hosni Mubarak talked Abbas into surrendering, but not before he shot Leon Klinghoffer in the head and chest and dumped his body overboard in plain view of his wife.

Such killing of handicapped civilians, unarmed pregnant women, children, and even the elderly was not new to Arafat. Long before Arafat emerged as the PLO leader, his organization, the Fatah, expanded his political aspirations through brutality and violence because, in his view, "People aren't attracted to speeches, but rather to bullets."[16]

Take the Lebanon village of Damour. Here's a slice of history the media ignored as they mourned the loss of their pet freedom fighter. Yasser Arafat personally authorized the slaughter of more than 10,000 Christians, many of whom were literally butchered and "chopped into pieces with machetes."[17] Nor did the press report the use of captured Christians in the hospitals as "live blood banks for wounded Palestinians" even after "Israeli soldiers who captured these hospitals found bodies drained of all their blood and stacked, like cordwood, in the hallways."[18]

I don't suppose Tom Brokaw reported that one!

What about the 1972 PLO kidnapping of eleven unarmed Israeli athletes during the Olympic Games in Munich, as the world watched in horror; or his 1973 ordering of the execution of Cleo No'l, an American ambassador to Sudan and two other diplomats; or the 1974 PLO attack on a local school in Ma'alot, Israel, leaving twenty-one children shot dead; or the "Black September" conflict in which Palestinians hijacked four Western airplanes, blowing one up as it sat on a Cairo runway? I'm sure the press didn't remind you of those cowardly acts because they were just another example of Arafat's numerous and "inventive" publicity stunts.

Arafat's crimes against humanity could fill several anthologies, not the least of which was giving the green light for the current Intifada—a wave of unprecedented terrorism which has produced more than 120 Palestinian suicide bombers in the last four years. Could it be that several of those bomb-happy psychos were raised watching *The Children's Club* a decade ago?

And Arafat was awarded a Nobel Peace Prize?

What gets me is that three short years after receiving such a high honor which, I should point out, no pope has ever been granted, Arafat gave a speech in Stockholm blasting Israel. He said, "We plan to eliminate the state of Israel and establish a purely Palestinian state. We will make life unbearable for Jews by psychological warfare and population explosion . . . we Palestinians will take over everything, including all of Jerusalem."[19]

As Jeff Jacoby of the *Boston Globe* has said, "This is a man who inculcated the vilest culture of Jew hatred since the Third Reich."[20] He's right. Tell me, why hasn't the media pushed to have Arafat's Nobel Peace Prize revoked?

As I racked my brain for any explanation why the American media complex suppressed the truth about Arafat's life, I figured maybe they just have a blind spot where dictators are concerned. We've seen that kid-glove treatment with Saddam Hussein, Fidel Castro, and Kim Jong Il among other tyrants. But corporate greed—now there's a story they love to cash in on.

Remember Enron, WorldCom, Adelphia, ImClone, and Tyco?

Arafat could siphon off money with the best of them. Yet his greedy wife, Suha Tawil Arafat, was pictured as a *grieeeeving* widow as she "settled" for $22 million a year when she gave up Arafat's numbered bank accounts to the New Palestinian leadership.

SHOW ME THE MONEY

What gets to me is that billions of dollars were sent to the Palestinian people because of their impoverished conditions. As a side note, I believe the Arabs wanted them kept that way in order to have a sore thumb in the eye of the world and in order to keep Israel off base. Let's be clear about the politics here.

The world decided to help the Palestinians by sending hundreds of millions of dollars, yes, even billions of dollars to Arafat, who stole most of it and gave some to his cronies who have villas all over the Mediterranean. The PLO leadership was treated to the finest things in life while the people under them struggled to find their next meal. It's a scene right out of *Animal Farm* where the pigs took the money and told everybody else they were equal.

While it's not known exactly how much he pilfered, *Forbes* magazine in 2003 placed Arafat on the annual list of the richest "Kings, Queens, and Despots." Some place his stolen fortune at $3 billion. What we do know is that, according to a CBS *60 Minutes* report, Arafat "maintained secret investments in a Ramallah-based Coca-Cola plant, a Tunisian cell phone company, and venture-capital funds in the U.S. and the Cayman Islands."[21]

Now, about that "grieving" wife, Suha. She hadn't seen Arafat in the three years prior to his death. Arafat had been wiring millions to Suha who was probably shopping for the latest fashions in Paris while he was busy seducing a generation of children to strap on bombs, kill Jews, and die for Allah.

The minute Arafat landed in a French hospital, Suha interrupted her shopping long enough to pop back on the scene and feign a broken heart. We were not supposed to pay attention to her ample, outstretched arms while she grabbed another slice of the Palestinian pie. She should have been arrested and taken to The Hague.

No, this woman is nothing more than Milosevic in stockings, or Eva Braun—Hitler's mistress—or maybe Mussolini's girlfriend. She'd make Imelda Marcos blush.

Tell me why Suha Arafat is entitled to keep even one dime that was designated for the impoverished people of Palestine. Why should she get

> WHY SHOULD SHE GET $22 MILLION A YEAR WHILE THE PEOPLE LIVING IN CORRUGATED HUTS GET THE SHARP END OF HER HIGH HEEL IN THE FACE?

$22 million a year while the people living in corrugated huts get the sharp end of her high heel in the face? That money should be going to reconstruction in the Palestinian territory and the Gaza Strip, not another facelift on one of her many mansions.

Imagine what they could do with that kind of cash to improve their lot in life. The return of Arafat's stolen money would give the Palestinian people more hope than anything on earth. Think about it. Suicide bombing aside, about the only avenue the locals have to earn a living is to sell Elvis-like oil-on-silk velvet paintings of Arafat in the souks of the West Bank. Let the people have the money. Let it be channeled productively.

Why does the American media sit by silently, or worse, glorify this mass murderer? Because they hate the Judeo-Christian values upon which we as a nation were founded. Therefore, they vilify America and Israel and lionize vermin like Arafat. Which is also why they'll never volunteer to tell you what's been hiding in Yasser's closet.

PUSS 'N BOOTS

I found the secrecy surrounding the sickness that led to Arafat's death more than a little suspicious. I'm not alone. Many have whispered behind gloved hands that he might have died of HIV/AIDS. Considering the mainstream media's virtual blackout of the topic, the last few weeks of his life were instructive, as I'll demonstrate in a moment. Keep in mind:

- He suffered from a non-cancer immune disease.

- He dropped about a third of his body mass.

- He had a low blood-platelet count.

- He was not suffering from leukemia or other forms of cancer.

- He was flown to a hospital in France in which the leading HIV doctors practiced.

- And there's a report in the book, *Red Horizons,* that suggests Arafat was bisexual.

Bet you didn't hear that last item in the news.

Let's put aside the other rumors that he was a closet pedophile and stick to the facts. In *Red Horizons,* the former Romanian chief intelligence officer, Lt. Gen. Ion Mihai Pacepa, describes a conversation he had with Constantin Munteaunu, a general dispatched to instruct Arafat and the PLO in the art of deception primarily to hoodwink the West into recognizing the PLO as a legitimate organization.

According to Pacepa, Munteaunu had bugged Arafat's bedroom and filed this KGB intelligence report:

> I just called the microphone monitoring center to ask about the "Fedayee" [a code name for Arafat]. After the meeting with the Comrade, he went directly to the guest house and had dinner. At this very moment, the Fedayee is in his bedroom making love to his bodyguard. The one I knew was his latest lover. He's playing tiger again. The officer monitoring his microphones connected me live with the bedroom, and the squawking almost broke my eardrums. Arafat was roaring like a tiger, and his lover yelping like a hyena.

After reading Munteaunu's extensive narrative, Pacepa wrote,

> The report was indeed an incredible account of fanaticism . . . of embezzled PLO funds deposited in Swiss banks, and of homosexual relationships, beginning with his teacher when he was a teen-ager and ending with his current bodyguards. After reading the report, I felt a compulsion to take a shower whenever I had been kissed by Arafat, or even just shaken his hand.[22]

Frankly, what Arafat did or didn't do with his bodyguards means nothing to me, with two exceptions. If proven true, his chosen behavior would both shame him and put him at odds with everything he stood for. Why? Homosexuality is not tolerated in the Koran. Period. As a Muslim, and a macho terrorist at that, if word got out Arafat was swinging both ways, true Muslims would have stoned him long ago.

That's number one.

The second issue is even more to the point.

Imagine what would happen if the condom were on the other . . . well, let's just say that if Billy Graham had been suffering from sudden weight loss, been treated by leading HIV/AIDS doctors, and virtually all other forms of illness had been ruled out, you're telling me the media wouldn't turn over every last stone on the planet to tarnish his reputation?

The fact that such an explosive

> IF BILLY GRAHAM HAD BEEN SUFFERING FROM SUDDEN WEIGHT LOSS, BEEN TREATED BY LEADING HIV/ADS DOCTORS, AND VIRTUALLY ALL OTHER FORMS OF ILLNESS HAD BEEN RULED OUT, YOU'RE TELLING ME THE MEDIA WOULDN'T TURN OVER EVERY LAST STONE ON THE PLANET TO TARNISH HIS REPUTATION?

story was ignored by the press once again demonstrates that liberalism is a mental disorder and, worse, that the left-wing media is in bed with the enemies of our nation.

When Castro finally croaks, I'm sure they'll turn him into an international hero even though he was a brutal dictator for some forty years. You've got to understand how these people think. The left worship dictators because they themselves are into absolute power. They're obsessed with power—having it, grabbing it, and preserving it.

They live in a power-trip world. They're obsessed with their own greatness from the minute they wake up, especially the pancake-wearers. The instant they roll out of bed, they race to read the overnight ratings. Are they still on top? Have they increased their audience share? If not, they break out into a cold sweat plotting how they can crush the competition.

So it makes complete twisted sense that they'd love a czar, a dictator, or any left-wing tyrant because that's how they see themselves. They live in a world of tyranny of their own making. They tyrannize people below them. They understand that the environment they live in is based upon absolute power. Which explains why the media has such a high respect for the brute force of a man like Arafat.

KINSEY THE KONFUSED

As I write, I can't help but notice an interesting confluence of events that bears comment. While the mainstream news media was kissing Arafat's coffin and showing their sympathy for the devil, the Hollywood media was aggrandizing a sexual degenerate from hell, Alfred Kinsey. Once again, history has been skewered, this time by the keepers of the Hollywood media. Why? To lend credence to the promiscuous lifestyle favored by the left.

In the movie *Kinsey*, actor Liam Neeson plays the part of this all-time great pervert who was not only a pedophile and sexual deviant of the worst order, but a complete liar and a fake as a scientist. Naturally, both the film and its fan base among the Hollywood Idiots omit his flagrant interest in pedophilia. And, not surprisingly, they also overlook the gaping flaws in his "groundbreaking" studies of sexual behavior released in 1948 and 1953.

The truth of the matter is that Kinsey published junk science. Why? To justify his numerous perversions and, in turn, to open up the so-called sexual revolution. The fact of the matter is that Kinsey triggered the sexual madness we're now facing and should be shunned, not saluted. After all, he paved the way for today's sexual anarchy using carefully orchestrated, bogus science. It was Kinsey's published "research" which first proclaimed one in ten human beings are homosexual—a total fabrication. Most reputable surveys put the number closer to 2 or 3 percent.

This fraud also claimed that virtually from the moment a child is born, he or she is a sexual being with a capacity to enjoy sexual pleasure, including multiple orgasms. How, pray tell, did Kinsey come to know that? Did he actually conduct sexual experiments on babies and children?

Brace yourself.

Look no further than the groundbreaking findings of Judith Reisman, a Ph.D. scholar and researcher. She investigated Kinsey's files and discovered that "Kinsey solicited and encouraged pedophiles, at home and abroad, to sexually violate from 317 to 2,035 infants and children for his alleged data on normal 'child sexuality.' Many of the crimes against children (oral and anal sodomy, genital intercourse, and manual abuse) committed for Kinsey's research are quantified in his own graphs and charts."[23]

And yet Kinsey, with his false scientific data, is still revered as if he held the gold standard for all things sexual. Kinsey opened the floodgates of the AIDS epidemic, rampant abortion, pornography, increased divorce, and the sexual anarchy America faces today. He was so disturbed as a human being that this wacko circumcised himself in a bathtub without the benefit of painkillers in order to savor and explore the pain/sexual fantasy.

But, again, the masochistic side of Kinsey was sugarcoated in the movie celebrating his life. No, it was completely ignored, as was his frequent correspondence over a twenty-year period with a Nazi pedophile, Fritz Von Balluseck, who later was convicted for sexually abusing some 200 children.[24]

On a regular basis Von Balluseck mailed detailed descriptions of his various sexual "experiments" to Kinsey who, instead of reporting Von Balluseck to the German police, encouraged him to continue his research. Concerned that Von Balluseck's "research" might attract attention from the authorities, Kinsey wrote and warned Von Balluseck to "watch out" in 1956.

> **KINSEY OPENED THE FLOODGATES OF THE AIDS EPIDEMIC, RAMPANT ABORTION, PORNOGRAPHY, INCREASED DIVORCE, AND THE SEXUAL ANARCHY AMERICA FACES TODAY.**

Shortly thereafter, Von Balluseck was arrested and brought to trial. On May 15, 1957, the *National Zeitung,* a German newspaper, reported: "Today the court has got four diaries and in these diaries with cynicism and passion, he [Von Balluseck] recorded his crimes against 100 children in the smallest detail. He sent the detail of his experiences regularly to the U.S. sex researcher, Kinsey. The latter was very interested and kept up a regular and lively correspondence with Von Ballusek."[25]

But the loss of Von Balluseck as a primary source was a minor setback for Kinsey's pathological preoccupation with perverse sexual experimentation. According to John Bancroft, director of the Kinsey Institute in 1995, the majority of Kinsey's child-sexuality data can be traced to one individual: Rex King. This child molester, who was later exposed as having raped more than 800 children,[26] provided a constant stream of "research" over which Kinsey feasted and recorded in his notorious Table 34.

In a letter dated November 24, 1944, Kinsey wrote King, saying, "I rejoice at everything you send, for I am then assured that much more of your material is saved for scientific publication."[27]

He rejoiced? What kind of "scientist" rejoices over a predatory pedophile like Rex King—who "masturbated infants, penetrated children, and performed a variety of other sexual acts on pre-adolescent boys and girls alike"?[28] Kinsey, that's who—a sick man who knew no moral boundaries.

In her book, *Kinsey: Crimes and Consequences,* Dr. Reisman writes, "Table 34 was truly grotesque. It reported around-the-clock experimental data on infants and young boys. The Kinsey team seemed perfectly at ease when describing the extraordinary data: 'Even the youngest males, as young as two months of age, are capable of such repeated reactions. Typical cases are shown in Table 34. The maximum observed was 26 climaxes in 24 hours (in a 4 year-old and a 13 year-old).'"

Kinsey was a degenerate. Period. He disguised his voyeurism as fact and called it science. The reason the Hollywood Caesars sought to honor this disturbed creature rather than expose him is because the foundation of their sexual license is built on his teachings. He's their sexual guru. If he was exposed as the fraudulent Freud, what would that say about their endless sexcapades?

And, as adherents to a Kinsey view of sex, the Caesars of Hollywood feel free to justify all manner of perversion, not the least of which is the movie *Birth,* starring Oscar-winner Nicole Kidman. Here we find a some-what confused Kidman, who has about as much talent as a pin-girl at a bowling alley, mouth-kissing a ten-year-old boy because she thinks her dead husband lives in his body. In another scene, the boy strips off his clothes and joins her in a bathtub. Of course, the libs see this child-lust behavior as the zenith of sweetness.

I ask you, where did my sane and safe America go?

Not to the Clinton Library, that's for sure.

THONGS AND BONGS

Perhaps nothing best typifies the insanity of the American media than how they covered the dedication of the William Jefferson Clinton Presidential *Lib*rary in Little Rock. During the days leading up to the grand unveiling of this $165 million, phallus-shaped glass building protruding over the Arkansas River, all we heard from the news faces were boring reports about the extensive "star-studded" guest list, and that a rock band I never heard of would be playing.

You'd think this was Woodstock all over again.

Ironically, the rain-drenched November afternoon was a perfect metaphor for the library, given the fact that Clinton's record had been completely whitewashed. Just as Clinton's memoir, *My Life,* airbrushed his dealings with communist China and numerous allegations of sexual assault, so, too, the library excluded those pages from his pathetic legacy. Nevertheless, umbrellas in hand, a coalition of the willing assembled to commemorate the most morally bankrupt president in America's history.

But you wouldn't know that reading the press reports.

Even the speeches left me speechless.

Take, for example, presidential nonstarter Jimmy Carter. In his tribute,

Carter hailed Clinton for his "insight, wisdom, and determination." Adding that Clinton was a "great leader."

Carter went on to recall a ceremony on the South Lawn of the White House where Bill Clinton and the "leaders of Israel and the Palestinians all shook hands and pledged their commitment to peace." That would be Yasser Arafat, the monstrous terrorist, he's referring to, who, I might add, should have been arrested on the spot for crimes against humanity.

What Carter didn't mention was that Clinton was the first United States president to shamelessly welcome a terrorist to the White House for tea and photos.

> WHAT CARTER DIDN'T MENTION WAS THAT CLINTON WAS THE FIRST UNITED STATES PRESIDENT TO SHAMELESSLY WELCOME A TERRORIST TO THE WHITE HOUSE FOR TEA AND PHOTOS.

Even President George W. Bush joined the litany of praise by calling Clinton a "great man of compassion." Mr. Bush went on to say that Bill Clinton "led our country with optimism and a great affection for the American people." Well, yes, some might call what happened in the Oval Office "affection."

Personally, I'd call it trickle-down immorality.

Granted, I really didn't expect President Bush to point out that Bill Clinton was the first president to establish a legal-defense fund, the first leader of the free world to be accused of a sexual assault at the White House, the first president sued for sexual harassment, or that the Clinton administration had the largest number of cabinet officials to come under criminal investigation in our history.

You may argue that it wouldn't be appropriate for Mr. Bush to remind the sheeple of Clinton's depraved record at such a gala event. Fine. On the other hand, the president didn't have to bend over backwards to paint a rosy picture of the man who gave our nuclear secrets to China, whose poor judgment led to a botched assault on the Branch Davidians leaving seventy-eight dead, many children—after which he hid behind the skirts of Janet Reno—and who granted clemency or reduced sentences for sixteen Puerto Rican terrorists.

During Bill Clinton's remarks, the former president reflected that "the choices and decisions leaders make affect the lives of millions of Americans and people all across the world." Had Clinton been a Republican president, the press would have had an orgy rehearsing the conflicting stories over Ron Brown and Vince Foster's mysterious deaths, the Lincoln Bedroom "Hot Sheets Rental Program," the fact that he was the first sitting president accused of rape, the millions of dollars raised from illegal campaign contributions, the sale of burial plots in Arlington Cemetery to fellow draft-dodger donors, his appointment of the ACLU radical Ruth Ginsberg to the Supreme Court, his cozy relationship with known drug kingpin Dan Lasater, and the hundreds of last-minute pardons.

At last count, at least forty pardons were not recommended by the Justice Department—including that of fugitive Marc Rich who was wanted by the Justice Department for "allegedly evading more than $48 million in taxes, fraud, and illegal oil deals with Iran"[29] and who was, as of this writing, implicated in the U.N. oil-for-food scandal.

Dare I mention the $450,000 donation to Clinton's library fund from Denise Rich, Marc's ex-wife?[30]

Again, why were the media hounds silent?

As for the library itself, while there are more than 76 million pages of documents, forget about the mounds of evidence dealing with Clinton's perjury before a federal judge and grand jury. You see, his obstruction of justice, his impeachment, and his affair with Monica were shoved into a closet-sized exhibit called "The Fight for Power." As you might expect, it's highly critical of former Independent Counsel Ken Starr's Whitewater investigation.

The exhibit boldly asserts: "The impeachment battle was not about the Constitution or the rule of law, but was instead a quest for power that the president's opponents could not win at the ballot box." Really? Since when was perjury, lying under oath, witness tampering, and the obstruction of justice not about the rule of law?

Absurd!

The press still lets him get away with Clintonspeak.

Robert Appelbaum, the exhibit designer, told the *New York Sun* that Clinton's impeachment alcove is really more about "the politics of persecution and the politics of personal destruction" in which Clinton is pictured as the victim of a vendetta by the vast, right-wing conspiracy. I'd expect Bill and Hillary to play spin doctor with their sordid history. Keep in mind this is the same snake charmer whose bottom lip quivered as he lied to the country, his wife, his family, his staff, and now to those who visit this monument of distortions.

Thank God the American sheeple are not that gullible.

A mere 11 percent claimed Bill was a "good" president.[31] I'm surprised his approval rating is that high given the facts of history. According to a report in *Progressive Review,* the laundry list of Clinton-machine crimes for which convictions have been obtained include:

Drug trafficking (three); racketeering, extortion, bribery (four); tax evasion, kickbacks, embezzlement (two); fraud (twelve); conspiracy (five); fraudulent loans, illegal gifts (one); illegal campaign contributions (five); and money laundering (six).[32]

That, my friend, is the sad legacy of Bill Clinton, the history that the deranged liberal media has tried to sanitize. If the mental disorder of liberalism didn't have such a stranglehold on the press, they would have exposed this cesspool of activity instead of burying it.

My intention has not been to tarnish Bill's record. He's already done a first-class job of that. I care only for the truth to be told, not some sugarcoated distortion. While I doubt that the Clinton Library will enshrine a copy of this chapter to fill the gaping holes, nevertheless, the truth has now been preserved.

> MY INTENTION HAS NOT BEEN TO TARNISH BILL'S RECORD. HE'S ALREADY DONE A FIRST-CLASS JOB OF THAT.

SAVING SNAILS, KILLING BABIES

Arafat and Kinsey are dead.

Bill Clinton is no longer president.

Does this mean these men are no longer a menace to society? No. History teaches us that ideas outlive the thinkers who espouse them. Which means dangerous ideas can and do linger for decades, even centuries. The mental disorder of liberalism can be traced back to its Marxist-Leninist philosophical roots of more than 100 years ago. Islamofascism dates back to the seventh century.

This brings us to Peter Singer.

It's possible you've never heard of the man. Singer, who is considered the godfather of the animal rights movement, doesn't usually seek the headlines; his preference is to pollute the water of philosophic thought from his throne at Princeton University's Center for Human Values.

I believe he's also one of the most dangerous men alive.

What are Singer's "human values"?

Being the good utilitarian-exterminator that he is, Singer has been an advocate of euthanasia for years. He believes there is nothing ethically wrong with killing one-year-old mentally or physically disabled children. How does he arrive at that conclusion? This mental case said, "If you have a being that is not sentient, that is not even aware, then the killing of that being is not something that is wrong in and of itself. I think that a chimpanzee certainly has greater self-awareness than a newborn baby."[33] Exactly the rationale used by Hitler in his early years to exterminate the mentally deranged!

This explains why he defends cockroaches while the murder of babies doesn't cause this self-professed atheist to flinch. It also explains how, according to his warped view of reality, there is nothing immoral with harvesting organs from comatose patients or aborted infants.

Wait, his demented reasoning gets much worse. In an interview with Marvin Olasky of *World* magazine, Singer was asked, "What about parents conceiving and giving birth to a child specifically to kill him, take his organs, and transplant them into their ill older children?"

Any sane person with a diploma from kindergarten would know that sort of behavior is monstrous. Not the brilliant Peter Singer. He responded, "It's difficult to warm to parents who can take such a detached view, [but] they're not doing something really wrong in itself."

You might want to read that again.

And this tortured soul has a distinguished professorship at Princeton! But wait, we haven't reached the edge of his insanity yet. Olasky pressed Singer further: "Is there anything wrong with a society in which children are bred for spare parts on a massive scale?"

Singer: "No."[34]

What about sex with animals? As long as it involves willing participants, Singer says, "It's not wrong inherently in a moral sense." Which is why he has both written and lectured about "mutually satisfying" sexual relationships with animals.

Sex with the dead? Necrophilia?

Again, "There's no moral problem with that."

I can see why Princeton has this guy on its staff.

If you want to see where this fraud who likes to play God gets upset, just mention the word "Christianity." Singer blasts "mainstream Christianity" as being "a problem for the animal movement" because intolerant Christians "want to make a huge gulf between humans and animals"[35] with their notion that humans have a soul and are created in the image of God.

This explains why the Australian-born professor has a real problem with America's Declaration of Independence, especially the assertion that all men are endowed by their Creator with certain unalienable Rights. I hate to break it to you, but Singer's Hitleresque thinking has opened the door to a complete meltdown of America's moral center. Even as you read these words, gullible students are sitting at his feet lapping up his dangerous ideology of death.

For its part, rather than expose Singer as a modern-day Pied Piper of the damned, America's insane media has found in Singer someone to celebrate. The *New Yorker* views him as the "most influential" philosopher of our times. The *Old York Times* relished the opportunity to demonstrate how his ideas have cascaded down from the halls of academia and now permeate the public discourse.

> RATHER THAN EXPOSE SINGER AS A MODERN-DAY PIED PIPER OF THE DAMNED, AMERICA'S INSANE MEDIA HAS FOUND IN SINGER SOMEONE TO CELEBRATE.

The *Times* gushed, "No other living philosopher has had this kind of influence."

That ought to frighten all of us.

"THE WHITE RACE IS THE CANCER OF HUMAN HISTORY"

It's bad enough that the media chooses to canonize reprobates like this deconstructionist. What is especially alarming is that the insane media elite routinely casts degenerates in a favorable light. The mental disorder of liberalism has so knotted their minds, they can no longer see straight.

Up is down. Right is left. Out is in.

And evil has become good.

An exaggeration? Hardly. As I put the finishing touches on this chapter, I learned that Susan Sontag, a lifelong communist, radical feminist, and sixties anti-war agitator, died of cancer. I was at my kitchen table sipping my coffee when I learned she had passed on to her reward in hell. Scanning the various news reports regarding her caustic life, I figured that someone would surely put her hatred in perspective.

> SUSAN SONTAG, A LIFELONG COMMUNIST, RADICAL FEMINIST, AND SIXTIES ANTI-WAR AGITATOR, DIED OF CANCER. I WAS AT MY KITCHEN TABLE SIPPING MY COFFEE WHEN I LEARNED SHE HAD PASSED ON TO HER REWARD IN HELL.

If that sounds harsh, during the 1960s this human tick blasted the Vietnam War, asserting that "the white race is the cancer of human history." If her comment had been uttered by someone on the Right about an "ethnic" race, you can bet it would have provoked an outcry of "racist" or "hate-monger" by the news hags.

Instead, nothing. Not a word of criticism.

More recently and just days after the hijackers from the religion of peace slammed two airplanes into the Twin Towers, Susan Sontag actually praised the hijackers and criticized America! While thousands of families mourned the loss of their loved ones, this America-hater wrote, "Where is the acknowledgement that this was not a 'cowardly' attack on 'civilization' or 'liberty' or 'humanity' or 'the free world' but an attack on the world's self-proclaimed superpower, undertaken as a consequence of special American alliances and actions?"[36]

To her, it was our fault that 9/11 happened. Nothing could be further from the truth. What further proof do you need that liberalism is a mental disorder? Sontag, who had been a card-carrying member of the Hate America First club, went on to say, "In the matter of courage (a morally neutral virtue): whatever may be said of the perpetrators of Tuesday's slaughter, they were not cowards."[37]

Hold on. She believes there is nothing cowardly about slitting the throat of an unarmed flight attendant or murdering thousands of innocent, defenseless civilians? What a demented world she lived in. On the first anniversary of the 9/11 attack, she called George W. Bush's "good versus evil" and "civilization versus barbarism" imagery nothing more than "the jihad language used by the American government."[38]

Why was she sympathetic to the burka crowd?

Then again, why be surprised when she stabs America in the back? Sontag, like many "progressive" thinkers of today, believed that agitation is their main function. While espousing love, they are little more than a catalyst of hate; vengeful, insistent, and often violent neo-socialists like Sontag act as if they alone understand the deeper mysteries of life while all others are apathetic zeros.

And yet, true to form, the legion of fellow travelers who control the media offered endless accolades upon her death. Reuters called Sontag "one of the most powerful thinkers of her generation."[39] The Associated Press called her "a leading intellectual . . . of the past half century" and praised her books, while *USA Today* lauded her as a "passionate activist."[40]

Unless this habit of offering sympathy—yes, even honor—for the devil is reversed, we will collapse as a civilization.

THE SAVAGE SOLUTION

At the outset of this chapter, I told you the mad dogs in the liberal media have wandered over to the dark side. This explains why the national media elite and the Hollywood media machine applaud dictators and psychotic behavior without a blush. As I do in later chapters, I'd like to give you a list of effective solutions to this problem, but in this case I've found there's really only one effective strategy to counteract their influence on the course of history and culture: *Ignore them.*

Tune them out.

Don't buy their products.

Without an audience, their power vanishes.

That's right. Don't watch them, listen to them, or buy their periodicals, that's all. Instead, when it comes to national or world events, find an alternative source for credible information. They exist; you just have to dig a little. If you think changing the channel won't make a difference, just look at what has happened to the once all-powerful CNN. They drifted so far socialist, they could have relocated their studios to China.

Along came the Fox News service with a more conservative editorial position and, as small as the Fox network was out of the gate, they've stomped CNN in the process, outperforming them at every turn. (Now, however, Fox has moved leftwards, so beware!)

If you insist on reading their papers, watching their news programs, or consuming their entertainment, at the very least hold them accountable. Don't let them get away with falsehoods and fabrications. When you catch the media rewriting history or manipulating the news, simply posting an opinion on a popular blog site can stop the liars in their tracks. That's exactly what happened to Dan Rather's forged Bush memos during the election of 2004. Always confront lies with the Savage Truth.

As for an alternative source for news, a great place to start is my Web site:

www.MichaelSavage.com.

Where over 1,000,000 visitors each month get it straight.

SIX

HEAD OF THE SNAKE: THE ACLU

This decade is a graveyard for politicians whose thinking was molded by the myth of the sixties. As a result, a time may be forthcoming when the majority in this country will elect a far-right leader who will win office on a promise to protect Americans from the continued agitation, social upheaval, and abuse of our courts by the hard-left. Hear me. I am not advocating such an action. But mark my words: The dark clouds of retribution are looming on the horizon. My prediction is not as ludicrous as you may think. Let's not forget that's ultimately how Adolf Hitler managed to grab control of Germany and impose Nazism. He was *elected* to counter the growing influence and violence of Germany's communists that should be a warning to us.

Look, Americans are generally a tolerant people. But even American-style tolerance has its limits. If the callers to my nationally syndicated radio show *The Savage Nation* are any indication, millions of Americans have been stretched to the breakpoint by the anti-democratic, self-serving behavior of left-wing leaders and their communist/socialist-leaning front groups.

Liberals like to portray their desire for continuous social revolution dressed as a noble enterprise. Wearing this clothing does not diminish the evil and danger unleashed by forty years of trolling down the blind alleys of "progressive" politics. And the people are starting to see the lie.

The sheeple will not walk around forever with zippers on their mouths while the left systematically dismantles our great nation and everything that gave rise to this shining enterprise of freedom.

That's a lesson the Netherlands is learning the hard way. As mentioned in a previous chapter, the barbaric murder and impaling of filmmaker Theo van Gogh by Islamofascists changed that "once liberal" bastion of tolerance into a different nation virtually overnight.[1] Blistering editorials immediately decried the slaying and demanded "a very public crackdown on extremist Muslim fanatics," including padlocking "unsuitable mosques" and expanding the "range of extremists to be kept under surveillance" while recognizing that "imams who encourage illegal acts should be thrown out of the country."[2]

You better read that again. We're not talking about a clampdown by a dictator here. This call to throw Muslim hardliners out of the country is coming from the heart and soul of Europe's liberal center.

Granted, if such a reaction happened here, the leader who might arise in America from the hard-right won't have any of Hitler's racist qualities. And yet extremism in any of its varied forms threatens our democracy and should be avoided at all costs. As I'll demonstrate in a moment, the times are ripe for the pendulum of history to swing hard-right. If it does, watch out.

> YOU SEE, THE LEFT HAS PLACED FREEDOM-LOVING, GOD-FEARING PEOPLE IN A STRAIGHTJACKET.

You see, the left has placed freedom-loving, God-fearing people in a straightjacket. The leftist media conglomerates and their associates in lower learning have attempted to control our minds, our hearts, and our souls. They tell us what we can and cannot think, say, or do. They want us to check first with the ACLU before we open our mouths. Ironically, as they tighten the straps, they insist that they stand for human freedom and dignity. In truth, the left hates true liberation.

This explains why liberalism continues to poison the well of liberty. Just look at the wreckage the left has caused our children, drugging them into compliance, while bending their minds into perversion in the name of tolerance. Or their efforts to strip God from the Pledge of Allegiance, while jack hammering the cultural stones upon which this nation was built—the Ten Commandments.

At every turn, these human ticks snap the crosses from our churches and war memorials, and whitewash our Judeo-Christian heritage from the history books. I've packed two *New York Times* bestsellers with examples of liberalism run amuck. To ignore this enemy within is to do so at your own risk. Try as they have to silence me, I, for one, will not bend my knee to the hard-left.

These "progressives" are dangerous to your survival. They'll stop at nothing to silence those with whom they disagree, and they are relentless in their efforts to disrupt the free flow of ideas.

Case in point: the Republican convention.

BITING THE BIG APPLE

In the fall of 2004, Republicans traveled to the Mecca of liberalism, New York City, to hold their national convention. This was no accident. New York has long been a Demoncat stronghold. Karl Rove and the GOP hounds figured they'd gain maximum political mileage by showcasing George W. Bush's leadership in the war on terror against the backdrop of a revitalized scene of the crime.

Before you blame the Republicans for shamelessly capitalizing on the 9/11 attacks, let's be clear: the Dems would have done the same if they could have. Neither party is above such exploitation. That said, convention planners were well aware that they might face a repeat of what al-Qaida pulled off prior to the elections in Spain—a last-minute attack to influence Spain's election.

Not surprisingly, several weeks before the events at Madison Square Garden were to get underway, the federal government issued warnings that terrorists of the same cowardly ilk could be planning more slaughter against Americans. The Department of Homeland Security and the FBI repeatedly cautioned that both parties' political conventions could be targets. Tom Ridge warned, "Credible reporting now indicates that al-Qaida is moving forward with its plans to carry forward a large-scale attack in the United States in order to disrupt our democratic process."[3]

While both the Democrat and Republican conventions came off without a terrorist incident, "terrorists" of another stripe worked overtime to hijack the Republican gathering. Disguised as protestors merely desiring to exercise their constitutional right to disagree, left-wing agitators from a host of proto-violent groups flooded the streets of New York City in a bid to embarrass the president and to hog the national spotlight for their hard-left agendas.

The NYPD already had their hands full maintaining order in America's largest city—now they had to address the ridiculous antics of naked fools, radical homosexuals, socialist front groups, and other left-wing extremists clogging the streets. A week before the Tuesday kickoff, the news agency Voice of America reported, "Police received their first test on Thursday when about a dozen AIDS activists ran into the street outside Madison Square Garden. Bearing no high-tech weaponry, these protestors just took off their clothes and brought traffic to a complete standstill."[4]

Let me get this straight. Radical members of the homosexual-rights group ACT-UP stripped butt naked to draw attention to the Bush administration's alleged malfeasance towards the continuing AIDS epidemic raging across Africa.[5] And, while mooning small children and families on the sidewalks, these vaudevillian street performers protested the White House's refusal to forgive the billions owed American taxpayers by many of these same African nations. And this, after Bush pledged $15 billion to fight AIDS in Africa![6]

Talk about the insanity of liberalism!

The president could give ACT-UP the keys to the entire U.S. Treasury and that still wouldn't appease these frauds. Their *real* motive in streaking through traffic was to draw attention to their self-serving, anti-American agenda, all the while protesting the Republicans' right to exercise their conservative voice. ACT-UP wasn't alone. More acts of mayhem from a host of other homegrown pressure groups on the left threatened the social order.

While a number of agitators could be cited, I choose not to give them a platform in my book, with one exception: a group called United for Peace and Justice (UPJ). On the opening day of the convention, UPJ amassed 150,000 to 500,000 protestors in New York City (depending on whose numbers you believe) to denounce America's war on terror.

Here's the hypocrisy. As the media covered the demonstration, they failed to tell you that a long-time supporter of Fidel Castro organized this anti-Bush march.[7]

That's an interesting detail to overlook.

No, rather than expose UPJ as the subversives that they are, the *Old York Times* referred to Leslie Cagan, the national coordinator for this bunch, as "one of the grandest dames of the country's progressive movement."[8] When did being pro-oppression become "progressive"?

Had the *Times* been thinking of serving their readers instead of stumping for this socialist, they would have reported that Cagan has a long history of involvement with the communist movement, not the least of

LIBERALISM IS A MENTAL DISORDER

which has been her participation as a member of "the Venceremos Brigade, which has organized visits to Cuba for over thirty years."[9]

> CASTRO IS A COMMUNIST DICTATOR, A HOLDOVER FROM THE COLD WAR WHO THRIVES ON KEEPING HIS PEOPLE POWERLESS UNDER HIS IRON THUMB.

We know Castro is a communist dictator, a holdover from the Cold War who thrives on keeping his people powerless under his iron thumb. Cagan is both a fan and an apologist for this dictator. And she's going to lecture America on justice? She's going to blast Bush for crimes against humanity? Why not start by calling for justice and freedom for the Cuban people?

If she and UPJ actually cared about justice, they would have organized their march in honor of George Bush's liberation of twenty million Iraqis. But being useful stooges in the socialist pacifist movement, they denounced our military, they trounced our foreign policy, and they bounced on the opportunity to blame America first.

Author John Tierney notes, "As leader of the UPJ, [Cagan] employs Leninist and Castro-style revolutionary tactics consistent with 'Fifth Column' political assaults against the United States. Cagan is one of the most experienced and best organized architects of the war against the war on terror."[10]

Again, you didn't read that in the *Old York Times*.

While camouflaged as "anti-war" pacifists, Cagan and her gang more closely resemble hard-line Marxist-Leninists.

FEAR FACTOR

The right to protest is one of the cherished freedoms protected by our Constitution. But there's a difference between protesting a point of view and intentionally working to disrupt and intimidate those with whom you disagree. The progressive movement uses fear and intimidation to attempt to silence all opposing points of view. A host of such disruptions were planned well in advance of the GOP convention, as were the lawsuits against the NYPD for "brutality."

Like a bizarre game of Whack-a-Mole, these operatives popped out of their hiding places, made an appearance before the ready eye of the cameras, then ducked for cover before they were exposed for the seditious saboteurs that they really are. Not that these agitators had much to fear from the major media outlets.

Tens of thousands of them converged on New York City and actually met to discuss ways to "disrupt the [convention] and sabotage the message of support for our troops and the war on terrorism."[11] Many of these revolutionary Marxists belonged to the "blame America first" crowd, which views the United States as the root of all global evil. That, despite the fact that America has liberated, fed, educated, cared for, and provided aid and assistance to entire nations for decades.

I know how these people think. To them, the only good America is a crippled America. That's why they hate our military.

They hate our moral foundations.

They hate our independence and sovereignty.

They hate our strength of character.

And because of their hatred of all conservative ideals, these fringe elements sought to use the international media coverage associated with the Republican convention to stab our troops in the back. Never before was the difference between the two political philosophies clearer. On the one hand, Republican leaders, delegates, and politicians addressed serious issues, like the war on terror. On the other hand were the old and new socialists, jeering and attempting to intimidate conventioneers.

The *Pittsburgh Tribune-Review,* when noting the intimidation tactics by these protesters to thwart the democratic process, referred to them as "unwashed, bad-smelling kids" who "jostled delegates" and who shouted at and heckled and acted like "inmates of a lunatic asylum" while "shouting themselves into an unintelligible moronic state."[12] Using fear and intimidation to silence the opposition ought to have a familiar ring to it.

Think early Hitler. Think early Stalin. Think early Mao.

Think Castro. Think Saddam. Think Islamofascism.

Just as every tyrant and terrorist group has done throughout history, the hard-left intends to obliterate truth and freedom by first posing as progressive humanitarians and pacifists. Which is why I say leftist ideology is the driving force behind the enemy within our country. What you might not realize is how closely connected these modern-day Judases are to the monsters of yesteryear, as you'll see in a moment.

IT'S ALL IN HOW YOU COOK IT

My love for good food goes all the way back to my childhood in the Bronx. My mother, God rest her soul, was such a wonderful cook. Mamma Savage always had something on the stove or baking in the oven. Day or night, that woman could feed a platoon out of our little kitchen. I learned early on that eating was a full contact sport—the sauce always ended up on my clothes, always. I could never seem to walk away from the table without soiling my shirt. Still can't.

And so, with your indulgence, I'd like to turn to food as we segue into a slice of history you might otherwise find hard to follow, let alone swallow.

You see, the recipe for left-wing activism in America wasn't cooked up here. As much as the left fashions themselves as being *progressive,* they're not. In reality, today's leftist movement is made in much the same way as a sausage—it's a blend of fascist, communist, and socialist ideologies from twentieth-century Europe, with a pinch of Nazism, all ground together, yet retaining the flavor of its various parts.

Look, I don't want to get too technical here. Entire volumes have been written on the subjects of fascism, communism, socialism, and Nazism. But, for the purposes of our discussion I'll sauté them so you can see what the left is trying to force-feed you.

We start in Italy. Take Mussolini. Given the failed state of our public education, I imagine you might not know the difference between Mussolini, Tortellini, or Linguine. In March of 1919, Benito Mussolini established the *Fasci de Combattimento,* or the Fascist Party. He and his followers (who wore black shirts as uniforms) seized power just after the end of World War I.

> **GIVEN THE FAILED STATE OF OUR PUBLIC EDUCATION, I IMAGINE YOU MIGHT NOT KNOW THE DIFFERENCE BETWEEN MUSSOLINI, TORTELLINI, OR LINGUINE.**

As a young man, he'd been arrested for vagrancy, he'd been a rising star in the Socialist Party of Italy, he'd been arrested as a pacifist, and he'd worked at an Austrian newspaper until he was expelled from town. Disillusioned with socialism, yet valuing a strong, unified Italy, Mussolini used his strong oratorical skills to emerge from the ashes of his own youthful failures. Managing a complete about-face on his pacifism, he used armed squadrons to terrorize and silence those who opposed his new fascist government.

Under Mussolini, Italy became a "totalitarian" state with him as the all-powerful dictator. He controlled every aspect of national life; he even handpicked the newspaper editors to churn out his fascist propaganda. Nor was he above the use of violence to ensure absolute compliance.

It's been said that Mussolini made the trains run on time—by shooting someone if they didn't maintain the schedule. Such was life in a fascist regime. Either you did what Mussolini asked, or you were finished. With fascism, the people are ruled from the top down. There are no higher courts of appeals.

No checks. No balances.

No dissenting opinions tolerated.

You do or you die. End of story. That's exactly what we're seeing with the Islamofascist throat-cutters today—it's their way, or the head's away.

A close cousin to fascism is Nazism. Nazism is fascism with a racist component, that's all.

Adolf Hitler, Germany's World War II-era chancellor, brainwashed the Nazi youth with an ideology stressing the supremacy and superiority of the "master" Aryan race—a race which was destined to rule the world's other races. And, in keeping with his role as the incarnation of evil, Hitler demanded absolute allegiance to the Third Reich and the fatherland.

As you well know, Hitler nurtured a demented hatred for Jews. He blamed Jews for Germany's problems, he called for a boycott of their businesses, he expelled them from public office, and he systematically vilified them which, in turn, gave rise to his Final Solution: the extermination of 6 million Jews in six death camps—Auschwitz-Birkenau, Belzec, Chelmno, Majdanek, Sobibor, and Treblinka.[13]

As did its Italian fascist cousin, Nazism made use of violence and intimidation to achieve its political goals and to maintain control within the party. In Italy they were the black shirts; in Germany they were "brown shirts," or members of the SA *(Sturmabteilung),* the storm trooper paramilitary arm most active in the battle for the streets against other German political parties, to eliminate opposition and foster mass compliance.

Are you seeing a pattern here? These two ideologies (Nazism and fascism) ruled the masses by force rather than by the strength of their ideas. That's what we're seeing today from the illiberal progressives. As modern day fascists, the left intimidates, suppresses, and seeks to stifle those with whom they disagree. Just ask your college students what happens when a conservative appears on campus!

The other major political movement, which emerged shortly after the turn of the century, was communism. Like fascism and Nazism, communism was ushered in through violent revolution and mass terror. Communism as a political doctrine was based on the ideals of Karl Marx.

Drawing on Marxist thought, Vladimir Lenin reshaped Russia into a totalitarian state. From 1917 until his death in 1924, Lenin "created a regime that erased politics, erased historical memory, [and] erased opposition"[14]—much like what we're seeing today in the actions by the ACLU.

Josef Stalin, Lenin's successor, was Lenin on steroids. Dissident viewpoints were not tolerated. To ensure that communism became the official ideology of the former USSR, tens of millions were massacred as he established the Communist Party. Stalin's "disregard for human life was matched only by his consuming paranoia."[15] Communism, then, is about total control. Blind loyalty. Internal purges.

And no personal freedom.

Fidel Castro is cut from the same commie cloth today, which should give you some insight into those on the left who admire, support, and embrace Castro as if he had built a New Jerusalem of the Caribbean.

ECO-MARXIST TERROR

That the mainstream media is left-wing explains why the handful of right-wing renegades who occasionally surface dominate the spotlight, while the terrorists from the left rarely make the headlines.

The worst of this breed of troublemakers are the eco-terrorists. These fur-spraying, SUV-burning, lumberjack-injuring extremists constantly break the laws of civil society because they believe a) only their cause is *just;* and b) whatever methods they want to use, including destruction, intimidation, and murder, are justified.

And, the EPA—better known as the "Environmental Propaganda Agency"—plays their role by enforcing bogus regulations often based upon emotional science for consumption by the growing eco crowd. They claim that America is poisoning the air, poisoning the water, poisoning the world, and yet these naïve activists refuse to acknowledge that the principal degrader of planet Earth is communist China.

> THESE FUR-SPRAYING, SUV-BURNING, LUMBERJACK-INJURING EXTREMISTS CONSTANTLY BREAK THE LAWS OF CIVIL SOCIETY BECAUSE THEY BELIEVE A) ONLY THEIR CAUSE IS JUST; AND B) WHATEVER METHODS THEY WANT TO USE, INCLUDING DESTRUCTION, INTIMIDATION, AND MURDER, ARE JUSTIFIED.

The eco-radical menace is so great, the FBI claims it is the number one terrorism threat inside U.S. borders—more so, even, than potential new attacks by Islamofascists.[16] Using such tactics as blocking roads, burning vehicles, and detonating pipe bombs, left-wing eco-terrorists further strains U.S. authorities already overstretched by the real war on terror. Philip Celestini, a special agent for the FBI, says, "This is the most vexing and troublesome issue that the FBI investigates."[17]

What does this band of left-wing terrorists seek to accomplish?

They are not concerned with the environment, that's number one. They want to destroy capitalism. They want to replace our system with a socialist or communist form of government. According to the Council on Foreign Relations, the eco-left does this "because they see most civilians as suffering from capitalist exploitation," therefore "left-wing terrorists sometimes focus . . . on such tactics as kidnapping tycoons or bombing monuments."[18]

They would even kill a human to save a snail darter.

Eco-fascism is dangerous to America's future precisely because it is so foreign to our ideals. Its followers hold no regard for what has made our society the envy of the world. Leftist ideology, eco or otherwise, is not just a harmless extension of the right of Americans to engage in political discourse.

They don't want a dialogue; they want dominion.

History repeatedly demonstrates that left-wing ideology is *the* primary tool to stifle freedom, capitalism, and democracy.

THE FOURTH REICH?

The eco-fascist storm troopers trampling through your neighborhood are flanked by a cadre of hard-left lawyers and activists. You'll recognize some of them by name, though you may not readily see them as the kind of threat I've described.

The head of the snake is the American Civil Liberties Union (ACLU), which fashions itself as the *de facto* Fourth Branch of Government. Joining their ranks is the National Lawyers Guild (NLG), MoveOn.org, People for the American Way, Americans for Separation of Church and State, Planned Parenthood, the National Education Association, and National People's Action.

And believe me when I say, they are out to refashion the face of America into a nation consistent with their socio-fascist leanings. How? By court-enforced mandate, as they have already proven. Many of these groups are funded by leftist pots of gold like the Tides Foundation, the Ben & Jerry's Foundation, and the MacArthur, Ford, and Rockefeller Foundations.

They also benefit from taxpayer dollars!

Using American courts, these hard-left groups agitate via judicial activism, overturning established law and the popular will of the people. They use litigation and legal threats as a fourth branch of government, showing no respect for true democracy when they seek to impose their left-wing agenda on the country. As such, they are enemies of democracy, not advocates of it.

> **USING AMERICAN COURTS, THESE HARD-LEFT GROUPS AGITATE VIA JUDICIAL ACTIVISM, OVERTURNING ESTABLISHED LAW AND THE POPULAR WILL OF THE PEOPLE.**

The ACLU is the largest and the most notorious of the bunch. With an annual budget of nearly $50 million[19] and fifty-three affiliate offices,[20] some 400,000 "members and supporters"[21] have been mobilized to do their bidding. From defending pedophiles *pro bono,* to protesting Defense of Marriage Amendments, the ACLU files upwards of 6,000 lawsuits annually.[22]

In the past decade alone, using their Gestapo-like pressure, the ACLU has managed to nearly wipe out any vestige of Christianity in the logos, flags, and symbols of local governments; they've eliminated any references to God in public schools; and, like good Marxists, they've attacked the Ten Commandments wherever they are posted, even when they are a part of a historical display in a public building.

These are "civil libertarians"? *Libertarian,* for the slow of mind, refers to freedom, not despotism and cultural destruction.

That's just for starters.

The ACLU urged the U.S. Supreme Court to uphold a Ninth Circuit Court of Appeals decision which ruled that the phrase "under God" should be removed from the Pledge of Allegiance. The ACLU works on "more lesbian and gay related litigation and legislation than any other organization in the country,"[23] and is aggressively working on behalf of same-sex couples who want to be recognized as "traditional" married couples. These human obscenities have also used the courts to overturn laws which were put in place to protect children from Internet pornography and other predatory material.

Not surprisingly, these pro-death activists also oppose any laws designed to ban the most horrific abortion procedure known—partial birth abortion, whereby a doctor partially delivers a baby, stabs it in the base of the skull with a sharp instrument, then sucks out its brain to kill it. This is nothing short of legalizing homicide. To me it's analogous to the maniacal actions of the Islamofascist decapitations. Or maybe Dr. Josef Mengele with his Jewish lab subjects.

The ACLU further endangers American safety by opposing *any* government effort to combat terrorism. The ACLU has, according to Senate testimony, threatened to sue any airline that deviates from so-called "random screening," meaning, most likely, a lawsuit anytime an airline (or government Transportation Security Agency staffers) stop-and-search more than two members of a single ethnic group in a row—except whites, I presume.

Likewise, the National Lawyers Guild, which is the incestuous cousin of the ACLU in terms of left-wing extremism, takes sides with our terrorist enemies. How? By condemning the Bush administration's right to use necessary means to extract information from al-Qaida and Taliban suspects held at Guantanamo Bay, Cuba.

The ACLU megalomaniacs and would-be ayatollahs have dismantled America's traditions with impunity far

> **THE ACLU MEGALOMANIACS AND WOULD-BE AYATOLLAHS HAVE DISMANTLED AMERICA'S TRADITIONS WITH IMPUNITY FAR TOO LONG.**

too long. This must stop! You cannot let them get away with this wholesale theft of our national identity. How?

Fight fire with fire.

THE SAVAGE SOLUTION

If America is to avert this coming storm—more specifically, a right-wing extremist takeover of our government like the one we're just beginning to see in the Netherlands—she has two options. One option is for Lady Liberty to surrender to the ACLU, lock, stock, and Constitution. After handing them the keys, we outlaw the Bible and the Torah.

Naturally, a card-carrying canary is immediately placed on the board of every school, church, and business to ensure all activities are consistent with the new national motto: One Nation Under RDDBs.

The other route, however, is the only way to prevent the winds of insanity from blowing across America. We must pursue direct, non-violent, action against the left-wing pressure groups. Start by revoking their non-profit, tax-exempt status. The taxpayer should not be subsidizing lawyers who, in turn, use their tax-exempt dollars to shred the Constitution and spit on the flag.

Second, seek out and financially support legitimate legal societies that actually uphold the Constitution. While none of these allies come close to matching the size of the ACLU membership, there are a number of top-notch conservative law and public policy groups committed to preserving our freedoms.

The successes of the socialist front groups are largely due to the fact that their supporters understand you don't get something for nothing. You have to put in the hours. You have to put in the cash. It's about time our side anted up.

Third, support the training of conservative lawyers in the specific fields of free speech, religious liberty, and Equal Access litigation, among other facets of the law. For years, the other side has groomed young attorneys with their hard-left ideology; our side has dropped the ball on that one. The Alliance Defense Fund's National Litigation Academy is one such first-class outfit.

Fourth, read, read, and read to know your enemy. Learn everything there is to know about her, her strategy, and the techniques she employs to trash our values. Of course, my two best-selling books should be at the top of your reading list.

Then, read Sun Tzu's *The Art of War*. You'll learn how to view and out-maneuver the enemy. Likewise, an incredible breadth of knowledge is to be gained by reading the classic *The Prince* by Niccolo Machiavelli. Although written in the fifteen hundreds, his insight will help you defeat the RDDBs at their own game.

You see, the left views us as unenlightened, under-educated, overly God-worshiping suckers. They're counting on us to sit on our behinds watching grown men in tight pants knock a football around the field rather than turning off the damn TV long enough to see their end game.

The last solution is not for the faint of heart.

This will take time, money, expertise, and perseverance. I believe it's time for the heads of the ACLU, the NLG, MoveOn.org, and all other left-wing agitation groups who are using the courts to impose their will on the sheeple to be prosecuted under the federal RICO statutes

> I BELIEVE IT'S TIME FOR THE HEADS OF . . . LEFT-WING AGITATION GROUPS WHO ARE USING THE COURTS TO IMPOSE THEIR WILL ON THE SHEEPLE TO BE PROSECUTED UNDER THE FEDERAL RICO STATUTES.

(Racketeer Influenced and Corrupt Organizations). I'm not a legal expert, but from what I've read on the topic, that's not using the court system for *our* own narrow agenda; it's a proper use of the law to prosecute a practice of improperly manipulating the law.

I'll explain.

RICO was passed in 1970 originally as a tool for federal law enforcement to nail the Mafia. But, during the mid-1980s, a number of shrewd civil lawyers read the fine print of the RICO Act. Section 1964(c) contains a provision that allows for civil action by anyone who suffers harm either at work or home as a result of a RICO violation. Huge fines were awarded—up to three times actual damages, plus fees. When news of that kind of windfall circulated, RICO suddenly became a useful tool in a wide range of civil cases, not just nabbing the mob. Fraud, breach of contracts, manufacturing defects—a case was made using RICO.

These days, RICO is rarely used against the mob. Rather, its legal teeth have been applied to businesses large and small, political protest groups, terrorist organizations, and even Catholic priests. Herein lies the heart of how to use the RICO statute against the left-wing lawyers' organizations.

RICO can be applied against the ACLU, the NLG, MoveOn.org, and others who are funding these groups, *because* they *do harm* when they subvert the rule of law and run roughshod over the American people using ideologically-friendly courts. In effect they are extorting the legal system for their own gain. RICO law is entirely applicable to these leftist extremists.

Can't be done? Why? Because you think the ACLU is a "legitimate" group unlike the Mafia?

Guess again. The RICO statue covers illegitimate *and* legitimate enterprises, which is why the law has not been strictly applied just to the Mafia or other illegal groups. Also, a RICO-defined enterprise doesn't have to be economically motivated—as in laundering money or pushing drugs—to be a target. An enterprise that pushes non-economic goods, such as ideas, can be prosecuted (see the *National Organization for Women, Inc. v. Scheidler,* 510 U.S. 249 [1993], for an example).

This all fits:

A. These left-wing lawyer guilds constitute "legitimate" enterprises (in that they are real organizations operating legally) even if their tactics are improper and subject to reprimand;

B. While they don't appear to be economically motivated, they are driven by a left-wing ideology which harms our borders, language, and culture; and,

C. Their defense of late-term abortion undeniably causes harm— death to be specific—to millions of children, which instantly qualifies them as a RICO case.

You may think I've gone too far. I haven't. I just don't care to wake up one morning with an Islamofascist/ACLU lawyer running my town! Nor do I care to see the hard-right overreact to their continual loss of freedom and, in turn, usher in an authoritarian leader of their own choosing. Both scenarios can and must be avoided.

Mark my words. The longer these anti-democratic forces are handed victory after victory in the courts by the left-leaning overlords, the more our system of justice will be seen as irreparably broken. That's when the hard-right will cry out with one voice and demand justice for themselves. I say use RICO now to stop the socio-fascists in their tracks, or brace yourself for the coming storm.

SEVEN

THE RED AND THE BLUE

The presidential election of 2004 sent shockwaves through the media, the Democrats, and the left-wing party hacks. Ever since their defeat, they have been scrambling to figure out what went wrong with their candidate and how they might seize power in 2008. So far not one analysis has come close to understanding the mood of the nation which ushered in this sweeping Republican victory. Leave it to Dr. Savage to explain exactly what happened. I'll do so by drawing a parallel to a personal story.

When I was a freshman at Queens College in Queens, New York, some pressure was put on us to declare a major. Truthfully, I decided on a major in Biology only because I didn't know what else to major in at the time. Besides, I always liked dogs. It seemed logical to choose Biology since I enjoyed animals.

During the spring semester I took a class in anatomy. Just before spring break the professor announced that we were going to dissect a fetal pig. Now, a fetal pig, as you well know, is an unborn piglet. My instructor gave each of us a piglet marinated in formaldehyde along with a dissecting kit. He told us to take it home and work on it over the mid-semester break.

LIBERALISM IS A MENTAL DISORDER

So, I'm walking home carrying the piglet in a plastic bag. As I was walking, I started to wonder, *Where will I keep it?* You know, under my bed? In the bathroom by the sink? Maybe down in the basement with my father's antiques? No. I decided to put the piglet in the refrigerator. When I got home, I tucked the plastic bag between all of the food my mother had in there. As I've said, my mother was a great cook, God rest her soul. Naturally the fridge was stacked with fresh food from the market. The meats, the cheeses, the this and that. She always had meals ready to serve on a moment's notice even if an army walked in the front door. That's the way she was. So I moved a few things around, putting the milk to one side. In went the piglet.

Later that night my aunt and uncle walked over for coffee and cake, as the relatives did back in my day. I was on the couch in the living room watching TV in my T-shirt. By then I had completely forgotten about the pig in the fridge. That's when my aunt opened the door to the refrigerator and saw a pig staring at her. You guessed it. Boom! She let out a shriek! She couldn't believe her nephew had brought home a dead piglet and put it beside all the food!

Now, it wasn't actually mixed in with the food, nor was it touching anything. But I'll tell you it was a real shocker nonetheless. Why? She had never seen a baby pig in the refrigerator. That's number one. Second, what I hadn't counted on was that the smell of the formaldehyde would seep out of the plastic bag and permeate the refrigerator.

You may be wondering what a piglet has to do with the election of 2004. Answer: The mental disorder of liberalism is like the fetal pig. It's as misplaced in America as the piglet was in my mother's refrigerator. Worse, the presence of this disorder has permeated almost all that is good within our country. Americans could smell this and showed up in record numbers at the ballot box to toss the liberal bums out on their priggish snouts.

We the People reaffirmed our faith in freedom. We made it clear that we want our country safe from the invasion of Islamofascism. Contrary to the appeasers on the left, we remembered that our fathers and grandfathers fought in World War II and stopped Hitler dead in his tracks. We longed for a true leader today who would annihilate these retro-Hitlers in headhoods before they

> WE LONGED FOR A TRUE LEADER TODAY WHO WOULD ANNIHILATE THESE RETRO-HITLERS IN HEADHOODS BEFORE THEY RAKE A SWORD ACROSS OUR THROATS.

rake a sword across our throats. The election was a rejection of limp-wristed pacifism and proved that Americans crave a new nationalism.

We want our borders closed.

We want our language—English—undiluted.

We want our culture defended.

We want traditional marriage protected.

Which is why I say, Mr. Bush, if this message in a bottle floats up the Potomac to the White House, please don't disappoint your conservative base. Forget about the Demoncats' sudden push for unity and their "let's all get together" nonsense. John Kerry did everything in his power to carve us into two jagged pieces. He spent two years dividing America. He shredded the oneness we shared in this country after the attacks of 9/11. And the minute Kerry lost, he had the gall to get up before the microphones and speak longingly of national unity.

Then, as we've come to expect from John Kerry, who suffers an acute case of the disorder of liberalism, he flip-flopped. Two short months after his call to solidarity, the most liberal member of the Senate was back on the road stirring up division.[1] Kerry picked Martin Luther King Jr. Day to whine, "Thousands of people were suppressed in the effort to vote. In

Democratic districts it took people four, five, eleven hours to vote, while Republicans went through in ten minutes."[2]

> IF THE KERRY LIBERALS FROM BEACON HILL HAD WON, DO YOU THINK WE'D BE HEARING ALL OF THIS TALK ABOUT UNIFYING THE COUNTRY FROM THEM?

On one hand he lectures us about moving toward unity, on the other he stirs up hate. And another thing. If the Kerry liberals from Beacon Hill had won, do you think we'd be hearing all of this talk about unifying the country from them?

Mr. Bush, it is *not* time to come together. You have a mandate. There is no reason to reach across party lines. Your conservative base needs to get something for the hard work they've done for you. Let the people see that you really are the Texan with blazing guns. Show them that America can stand tall, that we're not going to kowtow to the radical forces within and outside of this country. Show them that we don't need to live in the fear of ending up dead, like van Gogh's grand-nephew did in Holland with a knife pinned to his chest.

Mr. Bush, in your inaugural address you declared to the world, "We will defend ourselves and our friends by force of arms when necessary" and that you will "protect this nation and its people against further attacks and emerging threats." If you are serious, we want you to start by closing our borders!

Yes, we are living in dangerous times. As you said, "The survival of liberty in our land increasingly depends on the success of liberty in other lands . . . so it is the policy of the United States to seek and support the growth of democratic movements . . . with the ultimate goal of ending tyranny in our world." We know that, which is why we voted for you.

The left, however, has forgotten the 3,000 innocent Americans who were murdered on our soil, undeserving of death. The American people understand what is at stake—that's why they backed you. You were the only candidate who has shown the slightest inclination to taking on the psychopaths who are determined to kill or convert us.

Enough with the pig in the fridge. It's time to give the people some steak, not pork.

WHY THE DEMS DIDN'T GET TRACTION ON THE WAR

A number of things sank John Kerry. If I had to point to the top issue that returned Mr. Bush to the White House, it was our need for national security. Kerry's anti-war posturing after Vietnam positioned him closer to a George McGovern Democrat than a Harry Truman or JFK. In the end, Americans decided any guy who voted for the war before he voted against it was too confused to lead our troops in the war on terrorism.

Now, without going into the question of his war record or how far he chucked his medals over the fence, there are four other reasons why Kerry did not gain traction on the war issue. Let's start with the obvious: America was *attacked* on 9/11. Most Americans are decent people. Left or right, Republicrat or Demican, we don't like the fact that our fellow citizens— even if we don't personally know them or love them—were murdered by the practitioners of the "religion of peace." We want vengeance. That's a very human response.

You might say there is a real animus here to both defend ourselves and to get even. There was no such animus for getting even with the Viet Cong. We didn't even know who the Vietnamese were at the time. There were no Vietnamese restaurants in America. All you had was Chinese. That was it. You rarely heard of a Japanese restaurant in those days either.

And you certainly never met a Vietnamese shopping at the mall. In the sixties, no one really knew who they were. Today, there is video footage of decapitations accompanied by chanting to Allah posted on the Internet. We know who the enemy is, and we want them crushed. That's number one.

> **THE KIDS TODAY CAN DANCE ALL NIGHT WITH A PACIFIER IN THEIR MOUTH STONED OUT ON ECSTASY AND NEVER WORRY ABOUT WHETHER OR NOT THEY'LL BE DRAFTED IN THE MORNING.**

A second reason is that the Democrats couldn't stir up the angry masses of young people to protest the war. Why? There's no military draft to protest. The kids today can dance all night with a pacifier in their mouth stoned out on Ecstasy and never worry about whether or not they'll be drafted in the morning. That's why many of them couldn't care less about the war with Iraq. They figure it's a foreign war and no one can touch them. Why march in the streets with the old leftists and young crazies when there's no draft and so many people to fornicate with? So that's number two.

A third reason Kerry couldn't capitalize on the war is that his war, Vietnam, was a *civil* war. When Kerry attempted to brand Iraq "George Bush's Vietnam," the label didn't stick. Iraq was not a civil war. In fact, many Iraqis welcomed the regime change. They wanted their homegrown Hitler out of there. Granted, we've been in Iraq for two years. But the major conflict phase was over in less than sixty days whereas Vietnam dragged on for more than a decade.

Finally, this war is very different from America's war against Vietnam. How? The war in Iraq was not a unilateral action, contrary to the picture Kerry painted for voters. It has been a collective military action led by the

U.S. and Britain and conducted by thirty allied nations who were alarmed or even threatened by the spread of Islamofascism. To say that we must "rebuild our alliances" on the international scale was a myth and the people saw it as such. Americans don't want the French to pull us out of the mustard!

THE LAVENDER BRIGADE

Next to the issue of national security, a very close second factor for Kerry's defeat was something the national media will never tell you. John Kerry aligned himself with the radical gay agenda; Bush didn't. Here's how that hurt Kerry. For years the radical gay movement has been overreaching with their agenda. They pushed and pushed it all the way up to the U.S. Supreme Court. It wasn't enough for them that there's more gay freedom today than anyone—homo or hetero—could ever have imagined a generation ago, not even a decade ago. Americans decided there was simply no room for *more* gay freedom!

> FOR YEARS THE RADICAL GAY MOVEMENT HAS BEEN OVERREACHING WITH THEIR AGENDA.

Think about what I just said.

How much freer can you be than doing thirty men in a bathhouse with no consequences or public outcry—not to mention that everyone else pays if, God forbid, you contract a disease? Tell me, is there any more freedom than that? How much freer can you be when you're invited to go into a junior high school classroom and teach a boy to lie down with another boy and you don't get arrested—and the father doesn't come out screaming at you with a baseball bat?

Or that an entire high school, Harvey Milk in Brooklyn, New York, was built to cater to your proclivity. Or that the Centers for Disease Control already spends more money on HIV/AIDS research than on any other disease. Or that there are more homosexual characters playing on TV screens in millions of homes than ever imagined.

But in their view, America still hasn't done enough to accept and embrace their *liiiifestyle*. Now the radicals want to mimic and mock marriage. John Kerry was very much in their corner—and lost.

You know what this insane push for more gay freedom did? It motivated people who would have stayed home with their hat on backwards on election day to instead put down the remote and get out of the chair and vote *their values*. This was a watershed moment in our history and they knew it. They didn't want the gay movement to take over the culture. End of story.

The red states didn't come out *for* Bush *per se*. I believe the people who make up the bedrock of conservatism in America stopped voting years ago because guys like George Bush disappointed them by being too much of a liberal once in office. Oh, sure, Mr. Bush has a conservative label on his lapel, and in some areas he is. But on many other issues, as I've discussed elsewhere in this book, he's behaving exactly as a liberal would act.

That said, the people didn't come out to vote *for* Bush as much as they were voting *against* the invasion of radical gay militants who wanted to mock marriage and destroy a family institution. And while they were in the voting booth they threw Bush a vote. It was not the other way around. That's a lesson for any politician who doesn't get it. Stop wedding yourself to the homosexual movement. It's the fastest way to lose voters.

> THAT SAID, THE PEOPLE DIDN'T COME OUT TO VOTE FOR BUSH AS MUCH AS THEY WERE VOTING AGAINST THE INVASION OF RADICAL GAY MILITANTS WHO WANTED TO MOCK MARRIAGE AND DESTROY A FAMILY INSTITUTION.

Just look at the results across America. Wherever there was a Defense of Marriage ballot initiative, in all eleven states—even the psycho-liberal Oregon—the people overwhelmingly said: *Marriage is between a man and a woman.* They voted "Yes" in Oregon, "Yes" in Arkansas, "Yes" in Georgia, "Yes" in Kentucky, "Yes" in Michigan, "Yes" in Mississippi, "Yes" in Montana, "Yes" in North Dakota, "Yes" in Oklahoma, "Yes" in Ohio, and "Yes" in Utah.

"DEFENSE OF MARRIAGE" BALLOT INITIATIVE RESULTS		
State	**Supported Measure**	**Opposed Measure**
Arkansas	746,382=75%	248,827=25%
Georgia	2,389,344=76%	749,025=24%
Kentucky	1,217,857=75%	415,233=25%
Michigan	2,690,819=59%	1,900,578=41%
Mississippi	924,653=86%	149,854=14%
Montana	294,056=67%	147,927=33%
North Dakota	222,899=73%	81,396=27%
Ohio	3,249,157=62%	2,011,168=38%
Oklahoma	1,075,079=76%	347,246=24%
Oregon	979,049=57%	742,442=43%
Utah	562,619=66%	286,697=34%

If this were a ball game, the score would be eleven-to-nothing. America has eleven, the gay radicals have zero. Are you starting to get the picture? The people went out in some of these states knowing full well that Bush would not win in their state. Take Oregon, for example. There are many conservative Oregonians who don't vote because they've given up as they have done in California due to the lock grip that the Democrats have on the election process primarily through their control of the illiberal press.

And yet these good conservatives went to the polls to vote on the marriage amendment because they wanted their children and grandchildren to live in a country with some hope of retaining her former values. And, while they were in the sacred booths motivated to defend marriage, they also voted to reelect the president. Let's not forget that many of Kerry's supporters voted in favor of these marriage amendments, too.

Clearly, Kerry miscalculated on the notion that Americans wanted gay marriage. Nothing could be further from reality. Earlier, the *Old York Times* reported on the earthquake that rippled through the gay community when the priests and pastors in the Midwest didn't support gay marriage. So stunned by this turn of events, the homosexuals threatened to boycott local coffee shops. They said they'd rather drive out of state for a cup of coffee because they lost.

The radical gay community thought that they had the townsfolk duped. They thought they could spend Saturday night in a bathhouse and then put on a white collar on Sunday and Mr. and Mrs. Midwest would love them anyway. The fact of the matter is that the Smiths and Joneses detested such behavior and only tolerated the gays because they're decent Americans.

Let's stop referring to all gay couples as victims. Let's talk about the assault upon our culture. Let's talk about the assault on the most sacred of institutions, which is the marriage of man and woman. Let's talk about the assault upon our churches, which is the real fundament of this discussion. The red states could see farther down the road on this issue and decided not to tamper with what is unquestionably the best arrangement for children: a mother and a father.

Americans know full well about the need to keep a close reign on the fiscal policies, taxation, and a host of other social issues. But President Bush was reelected for the same two reasons which handed the Republicans a majority in both houses: *national security* and *cultural sanity*. It is suicidal to appease a fanatical enemy. It is insane to redefine marriage. When John Kerry didn't back a Federal Marriage Amendment he demonstrated how out of touch he was with this core value.

Look at what happened in Georgia. More than three million voted on a Defense of Marriage ballot initiative with a full 75 percent supporting the measure. Evidently, Kerry was so cloistered in one of his seven mansions, he completely missed what the majority of Americans care about. How else do you explain Kerry's unwillingness to stop this assault upon the family?

Which is why I say to the newly expanded majority in the Senate and House, now is *not* the time to sweep aside this issue. Mr. and Mrs. Republican Representative, you must give We the People in the red states some payback. You must carry through with your pro-family platform and pass a Federal Marriage Amendment (as President Bush promised in his State of the Union speech).

NUKING THE NUCLEAR FAMILY

War has been declared upon the family, upon the church, the synagogue, and upon every religious institution that we hold sacred. Whether you know it or not, you are involved in the greatest social/civil war in American history. You're living through it. Now, you can walk around with

> **WHETHER YOU KNOW IT OR NOT, YOU ARE INVOLVED IN THE GREATEST SOCIAL/CIVIL WAR IN AMERICAN HISTORY.**

your hat on backwards like a moron, watch sports, or play video games and think this is all a big joke, or you can engage yourself in this war—which is what I've chosen to do.

Just two days after 75 percent of Oklahomans overwhelmingly voted to reject same-sex marriage, a federal lawsuit was filed against the Oklahoma Defense of Marriage initiative. Matt Daniels, president of the Alliance for Marriage, says this attack against the will of the people is just the beginning. He anticipates "a tsunami of litigation designed to strike down marriage in different states across the country—including every state where voters approved state DOMA [Defense of Marriage Amendment] initiatives."[3]

Why do the left-wing radicals continue their assault upon this cornerstone of civilization? In spite of what they claim, it's certainly not about equal rights. Homosexuals already have all of the rights of every other citizen. They're protected not only by the U.S. Constitution, but by many other hard-fought civil-rights battles. It's not about property rights, because even unmarried persons who are not partners have equal rights in the joint ownership of property.

So what is this about?

It's about destroying the family.

Whether you know it or not, the radical fringe of the homosexual movement is socialist. Some are communists and, as such, they wish to abolish the family unit so that children will be raised by the state. That's the centerpiece of communism as articulated by Karl Marx in the *Communist Manifesto:*

> The bourgeois family will vanish as a matter of course. Do you charge us
> for wanting to stop the exploitation of children by their parents? To this

crime we plead guilty. But you will say we destroyed the most hallowed of relations when we replaced home education by social. . . . The bourgeois clap track about the family and education, about the hallowed correlation of parent and child, becomes all the more disgusting . . . by the action of Modern Industry.

You see, although most people see this as a battle to protect the dignity of marriage between a man and a woman, it goes well beyond the apparent. Just as radical ethnic gangsters espouse civil rights as their goal, using members of their ethnic community as soldiers in their assault upon capitalism and Western civilization, so, too, do the radical socialist gays use ordinary homosexuals as their foot soldiers.

This radical movement was handed a stunning defeat at the polls in November of 2004 not because the average voter understood the larger

> JUST AS RADICAL ETHNIC GANGSTERS ESPOUSE CIVIL RIGHTS AS THEIR GOAL, USING MEMBERS OF THEIR ETHNIC COMMUNITY AS SOLDIERS IN THEIR ASSAULT UPON CAPITALISM AND WESTERN CIVILIZATION, SO, TOO, DO THE RADICAL SOCIALIST GAYS USE ORDINARY HOMOSEXUALS AS THEIR FOOT SOLDIERS.

battle they were engaged in. But because on a deeply instinctual level they understood this is the final battle for the survival of the family camouflaged in the somber tones of the civil rights struggle.

Frankly, we could have predicted the outcome of all eleven ballot initiatives back in May 2004 when a similar initiative was placed on the ballot in Louisiana. Out-of-state radical money groups working in cahoots with in-state cabals spent *ten times* as much money as the churchgoers were able to garner in this battle over marriage. And yet the common man and woman went to the polls and voted overwhelmingly in favor of supporting traditional marriage.

But the radical cabals were not deterred. Shopping for a renegade judge, they found a real stinker in a black robe and, fueled with fortunes garnered from homosexual bookshops in New Orleans, these deviants managed through this rotten judge to overturn the will of the people.

Think about it!

One judge with his head up his robe in Louisiana eliminated the votes of all the citizens! If this is not the classic definition of tyranny, what is? Worse, the courts routinely ignore the will of the people by blocking what has been achieved at the ballot box. This oligarchy uses the gavel to hammer out reckless social changes that fit their neo-Marxist views.

You would think that the Democratic Party would have voiced great protest over the stealing of votes. If this had been a left-wing cause, they would have espoused great shock at the denial of voting rights. After all, this is their baby. One man, one vote. But when it comes to the radicals plan to eliminate the traditional family not a single voice of protest could be heard from the Democratic Party. Not from John Kerry. Not from Hillary Clinton. Even Al Gore had nothing to say when the votes of the citizens of Louisiana were stolen by one corrupt judge. You'd think this would be an issue close to his heart. After all, Gore kicked up such a stink in the election of 2000 over the alleged disenfranchisement of votes. He selfishly pushed his case all the way to the Supremes. But regarding this injustice he said nothing.

The only thing we hear from the Dems is that a Federal Marriage Amendment would, in the words of Ted Kennedy, "write bigotry and prejudice into the Constitution."[4] I say, shame on all of them. They're phonies, every last one of them. They look the other way while the radicals spit in our face and kick at the building block of all civilizations.

THE COLOR OF LIBERALISM

Speaking of the red states, the socialist left is made up of very clever people indeed. During the 2000 election they appropriated the color blue for themselves and pinned the color of communism, red, on the conservative Republican right. They did this for two reasons. First, the color red would have tipped their hand as to who they really are—the intellectual cousins of Karl Marx. Second, they intended to besmirch those who embrace the heart and soul of America with the color long associated with communism.

Look, I know full well that the elections prior to the Bush-Gore 2000 contest painted the parties with a different and sometimes confusing palette. In 1976, NBC color-coded the Ford states blue and the Carter states red. Four years later, ABC News still represented Carter in red and painted Reagan in blue. However, during that same election cycle *Time* magazine featured the opposite color scheme which they have stuck with ever since.

But I don't believe for one second that the newly codified shorthand of red=Republicans/blue=Demoncats is accidental. The left resents the fact that they've been exposed for the frauds that they are and, therefore, have used this little caricature to conjure up negative feelings against the opposition party.

Let's not forget the power of colors. From the infamous gang, the Bloods, to the Bolsheviks, red is understood quite well to be the color of revolution. Inadvertently, the left has acknowledged the force of the revolutionary power of Republican voters by consigning them to the color red.

Having said that, there's a distinct values differential between the two camps. We could argue that the Democrat blue represents the divide and conquer strategies of the entire left-wing panoply—pro-globalization, anti-war, anti-capitalism, women's rights, gay rights, minority rights, environmental activism, animal rights, anti-gun, and universal health care.

The Republican red appears to stand for the traditional family and the defense of marriage, less social-cultural pollution, educational choice, freedom of religion, fiscal restraint, pro-life, the right to bear arms, as well as an emphasis on lower taxes, an end to junk lawsuits, and a general patriotic support of our troops.

This working division is quite close to the truth.

> WHILE WE DON'T KNOW IF ELTON JOHN SODOMIZED HIS BOYFRIEND IN THE LINCOLN BEDROOM, AT LEAST WE ARE CERTAIN HE DIDN'T PAY FOR THE PRIVILEGE IN EITHER CASE.

Unfortunately, one month after Mr. Bush was reelected on a red-state, family-values platform, he invited Elton John and his boyfriend to the White House. While we don't know if Elton John sodomized his boyfriend in the Lincoln Bedroom, at least we are certain he didn't pay for the privilege in either case. I suppose on the scale of values that's a plus compared to the Clinton years when the Lincoln Bedroom was rented out like a hot-sheets motel.

I'm not sure who advised the president to honor Elton John and his wife-boyfriend with a reception, especially since two weeks prior to the invitation the Rocket Man called Mr. Bush "the worst thing that has ever happened to America."[5]

Worse than 9/11?

Nevertheless, Mr. Bush's move sent confusing signals; it blurred the red state values with the blue, creating a sort of pinkish America. While the Dems stand for a pinko America, I'm afraid the Republicans stand for a pinkish America; the differences are now so subtle between parties that one would have to look at the pinky finger of the politician delivering the message to see which side of the color wheel he is on. Just look at the immigration disaster which neither party will fix.

THE BUSH BASH

In light of the endless soul-searching by the despondent Democrats—many of whom are already seeking asylum in Canada—I feel compelled to further demonstrate why they lost the presidency *and* lost ground in both houses. Simply put, they still don't understand what America values. There is no better way to illustrate this point than to ask you to picture the following scene.

You've donated upwards of $25,000 for a seat at the John Kerry fundraiser, and you're sitting in the VIP section of Radio City Music Hall. The auditorium lights dim as the star-studded festivities of the night begin. The air around you is almost electric with anticipation as "Whoopee" Goldberg takes to the stage. Thunderous applause erupts from the sold-out crowd. You're clapping, too, but suddenly you stop. For a moment you wonder if Whoopee is sober as she staggers to the microphone, swilling wine from a bottle.

Now, try to picture your reaction as the human whoopee cushion slurs her words and launches into an X-rated rant about female genitalia and President Bush's name that could easily pass for the *Vagina Monologues* you may have heard about: "Keep Bush where it belongs and not in the White House." Without a blush, Whoopee jumps further into the cesspool by free-associating Dick Cheney's first name with that of the president's last.

Stunned, you lean forward and steal a glance at presidential hopeful John Kerry in the front row. Much to your

> TRY TO PICTURE YOUR REACTION AS THE HUMAN WHOOPEE CUSHION SLURS HER WORDS AND LAUNCHES INTO AN X-RATED RANT ABOUT FEMALE GENITALIA AND PRESIDENT BUSH'S NAME THAT COULD EASILY PASS FOR THE VAGINA MONOLOGUES.

astonishment, you see him laughing uproariously at Whoopee's tirade.[6] For her part, Whoopee wobbles as she exchanges places at the microphone with a string of celebrities. Throughout the night the audience is whipped into a near-frenzy as more filth, more hatred, and more anti-Bush rage is spewed from the pro-Democratic lineup instead of a single useful idea.

Imagine again: You watch as Jessica Lange calls the Bush administration "a self-serving regime of deceit, hypocrisy, and belligerence." You hear Chevy Chase, who fashions himself an intellectual, ridicule the president saying, "This guy's as bright as an egg timer," and quip that the most recent book Mr. Bush had read was "Leader of the Free World for Dummies."

Not to be upstaged, Meryl Streep sneers, "I wondered which of the megaton bombs Jesus, our president's personal savior, would have personally dropped on the sleeping families of Baghdad?"[7] And when dinosaur rocker John Mellencamp got his turn behind the bully pulpit, he says of Bush, "He's just another cheap thug that sacrifices young lives."[8]

Before the evening of Bush-bashing concludes, you watch a freshly-energized John Kerry sprint to the microphone to thank the participants for "an extraordinary evening" and, without offering the slightest hint of disfavor for the tasteless vulgarity of the lowest order, proclaim that "every performer tonight in their own way, either verbally or through their music, through their lyrics, have conveyed to you the heart and soul of our country."[9]

You might want to read that again. As if the night needed a nightcap, running mate John Edwards served up this wrongheaded remark: "This campaign will be a celebration of *real* American values."[10]

I've asked you to imagine this surreal scene because the video is not available. Why? Democrat operatives, who speak of "freedom of speech" and who frequently cite the "public's right to know" whenever they are digging around the records of the president, demanded an immediate and total media blackout of the Kerry fund-raising event in July 2004. If, as Kerry-Edwards claimed, their audience just experienced the "values" that are at the "heart and soul of our country," why censor the video?

Which values did they want to hide from the sheeple?

Despite the Democrats' efforts to hide the truth of their core attitudes and beliefs, they didn't fool the red states. Their posturing didn't pass the smell test. Their stench, like the piglet in the fridge, was bound to be noticed.

Even without the aid of this video footage, middle America knew John Kerry was the most liberal-leftist in the Senate, a wealthy faux aristocrat, and completely out of touch with the heartland. They elected a president who, though imperfect, resonated with many of the "real American values" which John Edwards could only identify with the help of a script.

What the Kerry fundraiser debacle demonstrated is that Kerry simply didn't realize how out of step he was. I've noticed this with politicians who don't know what the average American thinks. They constantly overcompensate in trying to parrot what they think are heartland American values. They portray themselves as men of the people, talking about their humble origins, blue-collar beginnings, and religious convictions. Who could forget John Kerry's photo op outside of a Catholic church after receiving communion so that the sheeple wouldn't miss his religious fervor. Such hypocrisy!

However, like John Kerry, these out of touch partisans are so enwrapped in the chrysalis of Washington, D.C., they have no contact with the real world—and it shows. Just listen to fellow Demoncat Simon Rosenberg, who thinks he's a leader, talking about morality. He called conservatives "a very formidable enemy" whose political machine "is beating us despite the fact that I think our values are more in line with the American people." Hold on.

Is Rosenberg right? He just said the Dems' values are more in line with

Americans' values? Let's see . . . would that be putting condoms on cucumbers? Telling eighth graders that they're really gay and they need their own high school? Shutting down the Boy Scouts because they support a straight, patriotic life? Suing business owners on false pretenses? Or does he mean jack hammering the Ten Commandments from all public displays? Removing God from our lives?

TO KNOW US IS TO LOVE US

Joining this call for moral clarity is Senator Ted Kennedy who also doesn't understand these things. He said, "We must do a better job of looking within ourselves and speaking out for the principles we believe in, and the values that are the foundation of our actions. Americans need to hear more, not less, about those values."[11] Really?

For my part, talking to the Savage Nation three hours a day, five days a week, gives me the most accurate stethoscope of the heart of America. There's not one politician who understands her heartbeat better than I do. So, what have I discovered about America's war over values that the politicians don't know?

I believe the election of 2004 and the run-up to 2008 demonstrate that most Americans are wrestling with this question: *Where should tolerance begin and where does it end?* In other words, how far can Americans be pushed with their kindness, their willingness, their openness, and their leniency toward aberrant behavior? When is enough enough? When will they snap? America is trying to decide that right now.

You see, while there is really little difference between the proclivity or *urges* of the red and the blue America, there is a vast difference in their *actions* and what they care to sanction. Generally speaking, the blue state/Democrat voters have urges which they have been taught are perfectly acceptable to act on in all situations. Their conscience has been shaped by the "Let it all hang out" and "Why not do it in the road" credos of the sixties. In other words, their guiding principle in life is: "If it feels good, do it."

The red state/Republican voters, on the other hand, feel the exact same urges and impulses—in fact, they probably feel them even more strongly because they *choose* to deny those urges for the sake of their own self-respect. They believe that restraining those impulses is better for their family, their neighbors, and for the sake of the nation.

> THE RED STATE/REPUBLICAN VOTERS, ON THE OTHER HAND, FEEL THE EXACT SAME URGES AND IMPULSES—IN FACT, THEY PROBABLY FEEL THEM EVEN MORE STRONGLY BECAUSE THEY CHOOSE TO DENY THOSE URGES FOR THE SAKE OF THEIR OWN SELF-RESPECT.

I sometimes wonder if the people who don't suppress anything get that. I'd like to ask them: Do you understand that the people who vote Republican and go into a church on Sunday morning have the same urges and passions that you have? That they struggle not to give into their urges all of the time? That they get on their knees and pray for the strength not to take the drink, to light up a joint, not to go for a meaningless one night stand that could wreck their marriage?

Bush got reelected because he understands this about red-state Americans and takes their concerns seriously. Which is a lot more than could be said of John Kerry. From the beginning to the end of his campaign, Kerry exhibited a hostility and a tone-deafness to these values.

You might say, then, that America is entering into a more restrained phase of American history—certainly more so than we've seen in the last forty years. This is for the good and might help the nation survive. We all know where the "anything goes" disillusion ends. Only by controlling impulses can we direct that energy in a positive manner.

Look at it this way. How do you train a puppy to stop peeing on your rug? You slowly but surely teach the puppy to control the urge to pee wherever he wants. Then, you teach him where it is appropriate to relieve himself.

> MANY ON THE RABID LEFT THINK THAT THEY CAN DEFECATE ON ANY CORNER OF THIS COUNTRY. THEY MAKE NO EFFORT TO SUPPRESS ANYTHING.

Unfortunately, many on the rabid left think that they can defecate on any corner of this country. They make no effort to suppress anything. From the flag to our founding principles, we see the waste products of liberalism deposited with pride. But thanks to the red states, the counter revolution is fully in force.

What, then, are the actual values of the average American? Are they akin to the vulgar, slurred, sexual exhibition of debauchery celebrated by the Caesars of Hollywood? Or are America's core values moving back to the Bible-reading, church-going fundamentalists that Hollywood fears and vilifies?

Contrary to the opinion of a leftist historian who labeled November 2, 2004, as "the day the Enlightenment went out,"[12] I am convinced only a return to a more austere moral America can save this nation.

HILLARY'S HOMILIES

The political leaders of the blue states know how to talk a good game. After the election when they discovered that Americans were still very much a religious people who cherish God, faith, and our Judeo-Christian way of life,

THE RED AND THE BLUE

the Democrats suddenly started to sprinkle God-talk into their speeches.

Take Jesse HiJackson. After the November election he suddenly reversed his collar to reveal the white and mumbled something about God, gays, and guns as being Democrat issues. Likewise, we were given a homily from the newly Catholicized Nancy Pelosi, who, before the election, was an invisible Catholic. Now, we suddenly discover, she had been a cloistered nun-like Catholic secretly practicing her deep-seated religious beliefs. I guess she was just awaiting George Bush's reelection to display her religious orientation. (Whether she will soon appear in a checked-school girl skirt and knee socks with an oversized cross remains to be seen.)

The sanctimonious Hillary Clinton is almost too shameless to mention. On the eve of President Bush's inauguration, she was found breaking bread in Boston with a group that uses faith-based ideas to address juvenile delinquency. Saint Hillary told the gathering of 500 religious leaders, "I've always been a praying person," and added, "There is no contradiction between support for faith-based initiatives and upholding our constitutional principles."[13] What's next, a book of inspirational messages? Maybe *Hillary's Homilies?*

Forget this sudden discovery of religion from the institutional Democrat left. Don't be fooled by their machinations. You must watch what they *do,* not what they *say.* If you want to really get a picture of their core values, look at their voting records. Study their proclamations. Watch what kind of behavior they applaud.

> FORGET THIS SUDDEN DISCOVERY OF RELIGION FROM THE INSTITUTIONAL DEMOCRAT LEFT. DON'T BE FOOLED BY THEIR MACHINATIONS. YOU MUST WATCH WHAT THEY DO, NOT WHAT THEY SAY.

There is no better example of this willful deception than that of the three-term Portland, Oregon Mayor Vera Katz, a Democrat who just completed her final term in December of 2004. On one hand she signed a Day of Prayer proclamation and on the other she applauded those who engage in a practice known as S&M. As I've often said, "Diversity is Perversity." This proves it beyond a reasonable doubt.

You're not going to believe what you're about to read. Vera Katz issued a proclamation declaring Leather Pride Week, which coincided with an event held by sexual sadists that included sadistic sex orgies and an event celebrating fisting. Mayor Katz's proclamation, which was obtained through a sadistic-oriented e-mail list, stated:

> Whereas the city of Portland recognizes the importance of a diverse community, and whereas the motto of safe, same, and consensual sex adopted by the leather and fetish communities is vital to all relationships between consenting adults. And whereas information, knowledge, and education are important factors in promoting and understanding and maintaining healthy social and sexual relationships, and whereas fundraising efforts benefiting worthy charities gives those causes further power to survive and flourish. Whereas efforts toward a healthy and better educated diverse community sponsors increased happiness, health, and awareness, therefore I, Vera Katz, mayor of the city of Portland, OR, the city of roses, do hereby proclaim August 3-11, 2002 as Leather Pride Week.[14]

The following are the titles of the events held as part of the Oregon leather pride week: "Fifth Annual Kinky Auction," "PLA Leather Tastings," "Erotica Show," "Men's S&M Play Party," and "Bad Girls Mixed Play Party."

Translating the lexicon of these sexual sadists, "play parties" are orgies in which participants engage in public perversions such as consensual whippings, fisting, torture scenes, and willing degradation as others look on. Sadistic play parties are often held in a host's basement, which is called the "dungeon." These dungeons are outfitted with numerous pain-enhancing devices.

Ms. Katz did so much to advance *diiiversity* in Portland that, after leaving office, she was invited and accepted a position at Portland State University as a "visiting fellow." Evidently, the college viewed her as "a regional treasure" and claimed "her presence will enrich all those in our college."[15]

While I'm not suggesting that Hillary Clinton has gone as far as endorsing S&M, she has attended gay/lesbian caucus meetings where she condemned the "discrimination and derision" from those on the right. And she's on record as saying, "We ought to be providing domestic partnership benefits for people who are in homosexual and lesbian relationships."[16] Clearly, she's pandering to her audience as needed. If her audience is into prayer, she sounds like Mother Teresa. If they're into the gay lifestyle, she sounds like Barbara Boxer.

And the Democrats wondered why the red states handed George Bush the election?

LIVING IN DENIAL, OR CANADA

John Kerry's concession speech called on Americans to find "common ground" and to come together as a nation. Right. After shredding our unity for two solid years he's a good one to preach. Evidently he didn't even take his own advice. During Condoleezza Rice's confirmation hearing for secretary of state, Kerry joined Boxer to become only one of two Dems on the subcommittee who voted "No."

Let's set that aside for a moment.

Here's one of the rare Kerry statements with which I agree. He said, "In an American election, there are no losers. Because whether or not our candidates are successful, the next morning we all wake up as Americans . . . and America always moves forward."[17] Not if the *Old York Times'* columnist Maureen Dowd can help it. This internationalist foot soldier wasted no time to blast the president. She claimed Mr. Bush "got re-elected by dividing the country along fault lines of fear, intolerance, ignorance, and religious rule."[18]

Does this look like she's attempting to find common ground? As you might expect, the red state/blue state debate over *whose* values will shape America's future can, at times, border on panicked hysteria, especially from the illiberal thinkers of our day.

> DOWD'S PERSONAL BRAND OF INTOLERANCE IS FOR ALL THINGS CONSERVATIVE. CLOAKED BEHIND HER PLASTIC SMILE IS A DEEP HATRED OF THE RED STATE VALUES WHICH GEORGE BUSH REPRESENTED.

Take a "scholar" at Poynter Institute who works to indoctrinate the next generation of journalists. He saw Bush's win as "a first step toward the theocratic fanaticism that has poisoned the Islamic cultures around the world."[19] Does he actually believe President Bush will invoke the powers of his office to proclaim a jihad?

For her part, Dowd's personal brand of intolerance is for all things conservative. Cloaked behind her plastic smile is a deep hatred of the red state values which George Bush represented. No longer able to contain herself, Dowd erupted into a boiling, volcanic-like spew:

> W.'s presidency rushes backward, stifling possibilities, stirring intolerance, confusing church with state . . . replacing science with religion, and facts with faith. We're entering another dark age, more creationist than cutting edge, more premodern than postmodern.[20]

Let's stop right there. What's really bothering Dowd and other fellow travelers on the left is that this president, who happens to be a man of faith, stood up to defend America against a cult of Bronze Age fanatics in dirty nightshirts. In her twisted view, Mr. Bush is a greater threat to America than bin Laden's band of throat-cutting Islamofascists.

That absurd opinion is shared by a New York columnist whose name is unimportant. In the alternative-weekly *New York Press,* this stooge for the radical fringe ramped up the anti-red state campaign with a cover story advocating that New York City secede from the union! He said, "For anyone watching history and thinking ahead in the wake of November 2, the secession of New York City from the United States of America is no longer a question of ambiguities but practicalities, not a question of why but how."

He's not alone. While a professor of history at Princeton was taking "full measure of the religious fanaticism that has seized control of the federal government," an unknown author was "hard at work drafting Articles of Secession for the Republic of California."[21] Then there's a Reuters reporter who scoured the globe searching for sound bites from unhappy international spokemouths who concluded that the world community fears "the most powerful man on the planet may do more harm than good."[22]

Another extreme measure under consideration by the unhappy political strategists on the left is to rescind the Twenty-second Amendment so that Bill Clinton can run for a third term. Clinton, in true narcissistic flair, floated this absurd notion saying, "I think since people are living much longer . . . the 22nd Amendment should probably be modified to say two consecutive terms instead of two terms for a lifetime."[23] Really? How would that serve the country?

According to the impeached ex-president, "There may come a time when we elect a president at age 45 or 50, and then 20 years later the country comes up against the same kind of problems the president faced before. People would like to bring that man or woman back but they would have no way to do so."[24] Clinton must think America lacks capable leadership. Why else would he suggest that we dip into the recycle bin?

From Jessie HiJackson to NYU professors, a host of unhinged Democrats and pundits were so angered by the outcome of this election, they descended into the conspiracy theory fever swamps and declared that the election was rigged—or suffered from voter fraud. Leading the latter charge was Stephanie Tubbs-Jones (D-Ohio) and Barbara Boxer (D-California), who almost dragged the nation through another painful and pointless charade.

It's not just the politicians on the left who are exhibiting the advanced stages of this mental disorder. The media czars are rapidly losing ratings, subscribers, and credibility because of their irrational commitment to a failed ideological position in a nation that clings to its core conservative values. Just from the point of view of survival—not to mention improved profits—you'd think leftist-bent newspapers, for example, would occasionally throw you an editorial bone. Do they?

> THE MEDIA CZARS ARE RAPIDLY LOSING RATINGS, SUBSCRIBERS, AND CREDIBILITY BECAUSE OF THEIR IRRATIONAL COMMITMENT TO A FAILED IDEOLOGICAL POSITION IN A NATION THAT CLINGS TO ITS CORE CONSERVATIVE VALUES.

Never.

They would rather see their newspapers fold one by one than alter their left-wing agenda so much as one iota. As a result, their circulations continue to plummet and their readership and influence are disappearing. Does that cause them to take the necessary corrective measures such as including an occasional conservative slant on the front page? No. They preach tolerance while exempting themselves from applying the sermon to their own pages, further exposing them for the frauds that they are.

REGRESSIVE PROGRESSIVES

As if you needed additional proof that these people are suffering from delusions of grandeur, a group of leftist billionaires led by George Soros huddled together behind closed doors in San Francisco after the election. They met to map out a new strategy to dump more, not less, cash to sway future elections to the left. They intend to spend at least $100 million over the next fifteen years to promote "progressive" ideals in what is called a "joint investment to build [an] intellectual infrastructure" that would encourage a "deeper progressive bench."[25]

In other words, they want to prop up progressive think tanks to dream up new ways to hoodwink the American people into buying their big lie. And they're not waiting until 2008 to get started. Interestingly, if Rupert Murdoch conducted a secret meeting behind closed doors with several other neocon billionaires, the press would have immediately accused them of conducting a star-chamber. But because Soros is a darling of the Leninist left, his clandestine operation was actually praised in the press.

Why are so many intellectual and wealthy businessmen committed to such a dying philosophy? Why do they remain fixated on a course that's sure to lead to their demise? I'll tell you. Their cult-like dedication to "progressive politics" is actually a substitute for long-gone earlier passions. You might say that such neo-socialist dogma is what too many sixties radicals have come to now that the spice has lost its savor.

Take Ted Kennedy who is stuck in the sixties. He still clings to the tired mantra that American capitalism is the heart of all of our problems and that socialism is the Great Solution. After all, Ted Kennedy is a diehard international extremist. We know that.

Frankly, I wasn't surprised when, in January 2005, he outlined his "new progressive" vision for the Democratic Party in the wake of Kerry's defeat. I guess America's rejection of the Democratic Party was too much for

Kennedy to handle. Evidently he felt the urge to single-handedly reinvent the party platform.

Incidentally, the "progressive" label Kennedy has so proudly embraced can be traced back to the Conference for Progressive Political Action (CPPA), which was nothing more than a front for left-wing, socialist ties. In 1924, CPPA picked Wisconsin Senator Robert La Follette to give leadership to their socialistic agenda. He, in turn, campaigned for a laundry list of socialist ideals including government ownership of America's railroads, timber forests, coal, ore, and oil fields, and power-generating water resources.[26] He was joined by the Farmer-Labor Party, the socialists, and a number of labor unions to form the short-lived Progressive Party.

That said, Kennedy may think he's being progressive, but he's just rehashing the failed ideas of a nearly hundred-year-old, socialist group. Frankly, after studying the text of Kennedy's speech, I don't know how he gets up in the morning and faces himself in the mirror. He's lost his way, that's all. He's forgotten we are a *sovereign* nation, not a socialist nation. I really think he believes America is nothing more than an appendage of the European Union—or at least that we ought to be.

> KENNEDY MAY THINK HE'S BEING PROGRESSIVE, BUT HE'S JUST REHASHING THE FAILED IDEAS OF A NEARLY HUNDRED-YEAR-OLD SOCIALIST GROUP.

Throughout his speech Kennedy viewed America through global-tinted glasses. He constantly referred to "global forces" and "the currents of globalization." He couldn't say enough about "this rapidly globalizing world" and "this era of globalization," not to mention "the global economy" and "global warming." He spoke of becoming "competitive again with international norms" and measuring America against "leading industrial nations"—will outsourcing our Constitution be his next proposal?

In Kennedy's America, all aspects of life would be regulated by the government; he would socialize all systems, programs, and benefits. Don't take my word for it. Here's what Kennedy called his "Medicare for All" proposal: "Our progressive vision is an America where no citizen of any age fears the cost of health care . . . we [should] expand Medicare over the next decade to cover every citizen—from birth to the end of life."[27]

Really? While the sheeple might like the sound of that on the surface, I have a question: Who's going to pick up the tab? A minor point, no doubt. But he's just warming up. Kennedy proposed the socialization of higher education by offering *free college tuition for all!* This neo-socialist actually said, "We will guarantee you the cost of earning a degree. Surely we have reached a stage in America where we can say it, and mean it—cost must never again be a bar to college education."[28]

What world is he living in?

While he's writing blank checks like a drunken Santa, Kennedy tells hard-working taxpayers we're not doing enough. Not even close. According to Uncle Ted, Americans should dig deeper for all college graduates who desire to pursue math or science by making "tuition in graduate school free for needy students in those disciplines."[29]

And Kennedy claimed employees "want workplaces free from all forms of bigotry and discrimination, including discrimination against gay and lesbian Americans." Again, what's the basis for such a statement? When was the last time Kennedy worked a day in the private sector? If he had, he would know there is far more hostility towards people of faith than people in the lesbian-gay-bisexual-transgender (LGBT) crowd.

WILL OUTSOURCING OUR CONSTITUTION BE KENNEDY'S NEXT PROPOSAL?

Are you starting to get the picture? Kennedy is for a bigger and more invasive government—one that knows what's best for the sheeple. I'm not buying it. There's not one new idea in all of this. Kennedy's "progressive vision" for America is nothing more than a reconstituted concoction of leftist ideology served in a new drink cup. What he's really talking about is no different from what the sixties radicals in academia have been peddling for decades.

Why, then, do they insist on pushing socialism? One explanation is that Sen. Kennedy and the Demoncats learned that they were unable to connect with most Americans on the issue of shared moral values, the war on terrorism, and of restraining the deviant impulse to redefine marriage. So, their fallback position is to dangle a basket of government subsidies in front of the sheeple; they promise the world free health care, school, college, housing, and more welfare, and tell Americans they deserve a break today while secretly raising the tax burden.

That approach is a mistake. It's been tried for decades. And, after forty years of pushing socialism, the people in the red states are wise to their game of Two Card Monte. If Mr. Kennedy and his party are to have a prayer of winning the hearts and the votes of the red-state Americans, they must first break free of the mental disorder that liberalism has bred in their ranks.

GOOD INTENTIONS ARE NOT GOOD ENOUGH

There's one other characteristic that separates the red from the blue states: The impulse against human suffering and the betterment of all in society (as voiced by Kennedy and the Democrats) seems to be what motivates many liberals. And yet they spend more time hating the oppressor than they do helping the victims. In fact, as we have seen in the last election, more vitriol was directed at George Bush than at bin Laden by too many activists. Hate is the essence here. While espousing love and compassion, hate seems to be their strongest of emotions.

While not necessarily having a faith in God, they still have the human need to have faith in something and that something is their battle against the phantom of oppression. In a way, it is a cowardly battle. For the truly oppressed are to be found in Islamic nations. To be a true soldier of liberation, as the red states understood, would mean one must volunteer to join the U.S. Armed Forces and fight against the oppressors of the "religion of peace" or vote for the party that will!

Instead of waging war on the "evil" conservatives in America, the neo-socialists should oppose the real suffering which exists abroad. To liberate the disinherited means to go where there is not even a vote; it means to fight for freedom where people do not have this right. If the true bankruptcy of mankind is to be found, it will not be found in this country. Urban poverty may be a curse, but global terrorism is a plague that threatens to annihilate all of civilization. The red states saw this and elected a president who would fight to spread democracy.

Poverty has and will always be with us. It is part of the human condition. Even Jesus said, "The poor you will always have with you." But the socialist left attempts to exploit this natural phenomenon by framing it as a result of class warfare. What they refuse to comprehend is that most of humanity lives in a drab and barren existence. No romantic notion of a perfect society will ever change that. The blue-state Americans who follow Kennedy, Kerry, and Clinton's lead may hope for a superior social system, but it is more likely to come as a result of lower taxes and fewer regulations than from governmental handouts.

Yes, while living in a new century, many politicians on the left act as though it is still the sixties. And, if you go back further, the sixties were derived directly from the ideology of the thirties. For those who never learned their history, the myth of the 1930s was that there would be a socialist revolution in America. So, the sixties resurrected the thirties, and the nineties under Bill Clinton copied from the sixties. It's a cycle of socialism that seems to run every thirty years, and with each cycle, the America we once knew becomes diluted.

In a strange way, the 9/11 attack on America by the Islamofascists in New York City and in Washington, D.C., may eventually be seen as the turning point where America breaks free of the chains of socialist oppression. How? Part of the myth of liberalism is the notion there is more peace, more freedom, and more equality under a pacifist/socialist order.

But the followers of Lenin and his modernist offspring were handed a wakeup call when the Islamofascists declared war on America. In other words, under the soft Marxism of Bill Clinton, America was weakened—morally, militarily, and spiritually.

Such is the fruit of socialism. And so, the lesson of 9/11 is that there will be no more America—capitalist, socialist, or otherwise—unless we defend our borders, language, and culture, which is the heart of the true conservative message.

There is still much work to be done. The enemy is not only at the gates; the enemy is at our throats.

> THE 9/11 ATTACK ON AMERICA BY THE ISLAMOFASCISTS IN NEW YORK CITY AND IN WASHINGTON, D.C., MAY EVENTUALLY BE SEEN AS THE TURNING POINT WHERE AMERICA BREAKS FREE OF THE CHAINS OF SOCIALIST OPPRESSION.

It is time to come out of your sleep.

It is time to put your hats on forward.

It is time to throw your pornography in a bonfire.

It is time to turn off your sports and entertainment.

You will not have a nation unless you awaken to the reality that America has become pacified, America has become feminized, and America is being compromised from without and within. You cannot let them get away with this.

Can America be saved? Is it too late?

I believe that with God's will and with your determination to confront the mental disorder of liberalism *whenever* and *wherever* it is found, America can both survive and thrive.

AFTERWORD

I would like to unlock the chains around the liberal mind. Whether you know it or not, as a liberal, you are a prisoner. For far too long you have lived in a cage where liberal ideas—and only liberal ideas—are expressed. It's entirely possible that you never meet or listen to anybody outside of your small circle of liberal thinkers. And if there is a dissenting opinion raised, which is very rare in your cloistered environments, the person offering that opinion is laughed at as being an eccentric throwback to a more primitive time.

In the end, your tolerance of the intolerable is actually a reflection of your loss of clarity; your tolerance of virtually everything and your "anything goes" attitude is not a mark of liberalism, it's a mark of the degeneration of your ability to judge anything.

Now, I don't blame you for embracing liberalism. I imagine you probably grew up in the same world I grew up in. But because you were so quick to embrace the seductive concepts of liberalism, you thought you had discovered something new. You thought you had broken the chains of oppression when in fact I can hear your chains rattling. The more you and those on the left scream about racism, homophobia, sexism, bigotry, this-ism, and that-ism, the more I know you are nothing more than a parrot in a cage mimicking what you've been taught.

As such, you are a product of our society. You've been brainwashed since childhood from the left-wing garbage on television, from what they teach in school, and from the behaviors applauded in the upper institutions of lower learning. And so I ask you to set aside the distortions and the altered reality of the left for a moment longer to consider the roots of this twisted thinking.

Let me ask you something: Why would a liberal call those who cut off people's heads and kill our troops and innocent civilians "insurgents" and "freedom fighters" instead of terrorists? Why do they judge America's troops but not the throat-cutters? Why are they so outraged over Abu Ghraib but had nothing to say when Saddam sent hundreds of thousands of people to an early grave? Why do they bash George W. Bush for the casualties in Iraq but not Bill Clinton when he dropped bombs on the Serbian people? And why does the left vilify Christians but then rush to give Islamists a free pass?

If you are going to let those in the asylum dictate to you what you should be thinking, you're going to wind up crazy. Which begs the question: How did the "leaders" of liberalism become so corkscrewed in their thinking?

The roots of their twisted worldview can be traced back some forty years. During the sixties, there was a movement in this country to change the way we looked at deviancy. Back then, we understood what a bum or a junkie or a pervert or a suicidal maniac was. Most of us still have a lingering memory of what those words mean. However, those on the left started to change the meaning of those words during the "permissive sixties" so that everything which was once deviant is now presented as normal.

Essentially, they've eliminated the concept of deviance and perversion completely.

For example, they've defused your strong sanctions against pedophilia by now dismissing that perversion as nothing more than a point on the "erotic continuum." Likewise, anyone in the past who tried to take their own life was considered suicidal. Back then, society tried to stop them—for their own good. Today, the mentally wacked-out liberals of this country have twisted assisted suicide into just another acceptable *treeeatment* that should be available to patients.

What's more, these Enlightened Ones have altered the rules of dialogue so that if you or I dare to remind people about the truth of their actions, we are the deviants who should be punished to the fullest extent of the law. And so, consequently, liberalism has broken down the moral boundaries of our nation and created a state of social disintegration in this country. As any thinking person knows, without social norms there can be no society whatsoever.

Can't you see what's going on here?

Now, why should you and I care?

After forty years of this agitation, America is experiencing what Daniel Patrick Moynihan called "defining deviancy down." I believe the timing couldn't be worse. We're facing an enemy more dangerous than Hitler. Why do I say that? Hitler was unabashedly evil. Everyone knew that. There was no ambivalence about Hitler and his Nazi Party.

But today, as we face a terrorist enemy who wants to kill us, the demented voices of the left actually defend and dismiss such evil—worse, the left blames us for their hatred. Because of the mental disorder of liberalism, America is being divided from without and within. Ultimately, such sedition sets the stage for the complete meltdown of our security.

I am encouraged that most of America has started to embrace this fact. The sheeple are beginning to arise from their sleep. They are starting to demand that the left stop pushing the anti-family, anti-Christian, anti-police, anti-military, anti-American stories in our newspapers, in our entertainment, in our textbooks, and in our schools.

Even where I live, San Francisco, a city that is in many ways the epicenter of the twisted left, I am witnessing growing signs of this awakening. Everywhere I go, people will stop me on the street and confide, "Thank God you're out there saying what I've been thinking!" Yes, I believe a day is coming when a return to what has made America great will become the dominant viewpoint once again.

This reawakening started as a whisper a number of years ago, sparked by those of us in conservative talk radio. And then it became a murmur.

That murmur has become an undertone.

One day it will become a roar.

However, this revival of a new nationalism must come sooner rather than later if we are to defeat the enemy.

What enemy am I talking about? Radical Islam is the enemy external. The enemy within are those whom I have presented in this book, including the ACLU, the National Lawyers Guild, and the entire pack of anti-family, anti-faith, anti-America deviants. Those are the enemies of our survival. Which is why I invite you to break free of the ball and chain of liberalism.

SAVAGESPEAK GLOSSARY OF SAVAGISMS

Baggy-eyed Bolshevik: Jim Lehrer

Briefcase Mafia: trial lawyers

Brown Shorts: radical gay activists

Bypassed Bolsheviks in Buicks: retired, retreat leftists, known to haunt Palm Beach County, Florida

Caesars of Hollywood: actors and actresses who move among us as if they were gods

Christophobia: the loathing and hatred of Christianity by bigoted, intolerant, secular leftists

Clipped hair, Mean-faced Women: self-evident

Coffee Cup Annan: the shameless, oil swilling leader of the U.N.

Compassionate Conservative: me

Condo Commies: wealthy socialists

Corned-beef Commies: unhealthy, wealthy socialists

Crack Pants: pants worn by skinny middle-class kids who emulate gang-bangers

Crescent News Network: CNN

Czarina of Education: the clipped-hair, mean-faced women who dominate the National (mis)Education Association and control it with a jackboot

Demicans: Republicans who act like Democrats (e.g., Arlen Specter)

Demoncats: a euphemistic term for godless Democrats

Dodge City of Talk Radio: *The Savage Nation*

Dungism: a school of liberal art

Empty Skirt: a pancake-faced, teleprompter-reading leg-crosser in a newsroom

EPA: Environmental Propaganda Agency

"from Boulder Dam to dental dams in one generation": from historic feats of engineering to corrupted acts of fellatio

"from kid gloves to latex gloves in one generation": think your grandmother, then think Rosie O'Donnell

"from St. Christopher's medals to crystals in one generation": going from traditional faith to New Age cosmic flakes

The Grim Reefer Gang: advocates for medical marijuana

Government-Media Complex: unholy alliance between big government and media elites

Headcutters in Headscarfs: evangelists who spread the religion of peace by cutting people to pieces

Hieroglyphics Set to a Beat: rap

Rev. Jesse HiJackson: pastor of the First Rainbow Church of Shakedowns

Hitler in a Dirty Nightshirt: Osama bin Laden

Hollywood Idiots: mindless thespians from the Land of Make-Believe

Houses of Porn and Scorn: today's "liberal" colleges

Illiberal: what "liberal" used to mean

Infidels: the Savage listening audience

Institutes of Lower Living: colleges where junior sheeple can get the finest illiberal education that taxpayer money can buy

Islamofascists: dirty nightshhirt-clad radical Muslims who walk with a Koran in one hand and a bloody, rusty knife in the other

Kneejerk Conservatives: reflexive right-wingers who never ask "Why?" when conservative leaders say "Drink the Kool-Aid"

Krapistan: any Turd-World dustbowl still stuck in the Middle Ages

Lexus Liberals: Kerry-brand liberals who despise the nation that made their wealth

Lunchroom Lenins: found mainly in Southern Florida at early, early, early bird buffets

Madeline Halfbright: former Secretary of Hate under Bill Clinton who, in my day, would have run a deli on the lower east side of Manhattan

Mayor Any Twosome-Noosem: S.F. Mayor Gavin Newsom who violated California state law by issuing thousands of gay "marriage" licenses

Mindsluts: news chicks who prostitute their ethics to espouse the party line

Mushroom Boys: L.A. screenwriters

Ninth Jerk-it Court of Schlemiels: the Ninth Circuit Court of Appeals, the most liberal federal court in the nation, where the justices have their heads up their robes

Nostrilman: Henry Waxman

Old York Times: the once-great Gray Lady, deflowered by "Pinchy" Sulzberger's juvenile worldview

PBS: Palestine Broadcasting System

Pinchy Sulzberger: the left-leaning czar of the *Old York Times* and son of Arthur H. Sulzberger

Pot in Every Chicken: legalization of marijuana

Psychological Nudity: exposing the Savage Truth

Rat Boy: John Walker Lindh, the so-called American Taliban, who stabbed America in the back

Republicrats: turncoat Republicans (John McCain and other left-leaning anticonservatives)

Red Diaper Doper Babies (RDDBs): psychotic sixties leftovers who mixed too much Marx with their marijuana

Savagettes: the babes of *The Savage Nation*

Sheeple: the unthinking, gullible masses

She-ocracy: the reigning rule of radical feminism that emasculated America's men

Socialism: organized crime with an army

Spawning like Shrimp: the swarming of illegal aliens at our southern border

Stand-up Stalins: anti-American comedians

"the stench from the bench is making me clench": the odorous rule of liberal judges

The Supremes: U.S. Supreme Court justices

TNN: Taliban News Network, also known as CNN

Trickle Down Immorality: as perfected by Bill Clinton, the course material in the majority of America's public schools

Yenta-tainers: gossipy, meddlesome, clueless female performers, *a la* BraBra Streisand or Barbara Boxer

ENDNOTES

Preface

1. "Mexico threatens Arizona over anti-illegals measure Prop 200,"
   WorldNetDaily.com, January 28, 2005.
2. "Mexico Threatens Arizona," WorldNetDaily.com.
3. "Hitler 'Ordered Pope Kidnapped,'" CNN.com, January 15, 2005.

1   More Patton, Less Patent Leather

1. Fred Weir, "Iraqi Defeat Jolts Russian Military," *Christian Science Monitor,* April
   16, 2003.
2. Weir, "Iraqi Defeat Jolts Russian Military."
3. "Official Says up to 30,000 Terrorists Are in Iraq," Associated Press, January 5,
   2005.
4. Lieutenant Colonel Tim Collins in a prebattle speech, March 19, 2003,
   http://www.usni.org/resources/Iraq/collins_to_royal_irish_guards.htm.
5. George S. Patton, http://www.specialoperations.com/Focus/quotes.html.
6. David E. Sanger and Eric Schmitt, "How U.S. Might Disengage in Iraq," *New York
   Times,* January 10, 2005.
7. Daniel Benjamin, "Condi's Phony History: Sorry, Dr. Rice, Postwar Germany Was
   Nothing Like Iraq," *Slate,* August 29, 2003.
8. Perry Biddiscombe, *Werwolf! The History of the National Socialist Guerrilla
   Movement, 1944–1946,* http://en.wikipedia.org/wiki/Werwolf.
9. Benjamin, "Condi's Phony History."
10. "Cole Guards Told Not to Fire First," NewsMax.com, November 14, 2000.

11. "Standing Guard with No Ammunition?" CBSNews.com, November 14, 2000.

12. "Iraq Shiite Win May Bring 'Super Iran': Critics," Associated Press, December 18, 2004.

13. John F. Cullinan, "A Republic, If You Can Keep It," *National Review Online,* March 10, 2004.

14. Burt Herman, "Afghans Get Constitution Draft," CBSNews.com, November 3, 2004.

15. "Cohen Seeks a Plan to Partition Iraq, Report Says," ArabicNews.com, March 8, 1999.

2   Unmasking Islamofascism

1. Larry B. Stammer, "First Lady Breaks Ground with Muslims," *Los Angeles Times,* May 31, 1996.

2. Robert Spencer, "The Rapid Islamization of Europe," WorldNetDaily.com, September 18, 2004.

3. "Muslims Torture Christian to Death," WorldNetDaily.com, May15, 2004.

4. "Muslims Slaughter 600 Christians," WorldNetDaily.com, May 15, 2004.

5. Winston Churchill, from his "Iron Curtain" speech offered at Westminster College, Fulton, MO, 1946.

6. Maggie Gallagher, "Timothy McVeigh, Christian Terrorist?" Universal Press Syndicate, October 28, 2002.

7. "Timothy McVeigh, Christian Terrorist?"

8. Barbara Ehrenreich, "The Making of McVeigh," *Progressive,* July 2001.

9. Raymond S. Kraft, "The Death of Liberalism," KGO-AM Radio Web site, October 10, 2004. The article—originally posted at http://www.kgoam810.com/viewentry.asp?ID=316609&PT=PERSONALITIES— was later pulled from the site. This doesn't surprise me. KGO leans left, and any message this clear and lucid was liable to be trashed. You can still read it, however, thanks to ChronWatch.com: http://www.chronwatch.com/content/contentDisplay.asp?aid=10276.

10. George S. Patton, *The War as I Knew It* (Boston: Houghton Mifflin, 1947), 49.

11. Lev Navrozov, "Social Influence of Christianity vs. Islam," NewsMax.com, October 22, 2004.

12. Robert Spencer, "The Mullahs' Europe," FrontPageMagazine.com, September 22, 2002.

13. All bullet-pointed items: Spencer, "The Mullahs' Europe."

14. Dave Eberhart, "Bodansky: Terrorists Seek 'Mass Casualties on an Unprecedented Scale,'" NewsMax.com, October 5, 2004.

15. Ali Sina, "Aisha the Child Wife of Muhammad," http://www.faithfreedom.org/articles/sina/ayesha.htm.

16. Taken from *Sahih Burhari,* Volume 7, Book 62, Number 64.

17. *Sahih Burhari,* Volume 5, Book 58, Number 234.
18. Dr. John Hagee, "ACLU Assaults Constitution, Promotes Islam," WorldNetDaily.com, August 30, 2002.
19. "Muslim Cleric Wants 'Women of Mass Destruction,'" WorldNetDaily.com, October 9, 2004.
20. The Koran, Surah 1:28; 2:161; 7:124.
21. "The Qur'an and Homosexuality," ReligiousTolerance.org, http://www.religious-tolerance.org/hom_isla.htm.
22. Christopher Caldwell, "When Bernard Lewis speaks . . ." *Weekly Standard,* November 4, 2004.
23. Austin Miles, "Federal Lawsuit Filed Against Byron School," ASSIST News Service, June 26, 2002.
24. Miles, "Federal Lawsuit Filed Against Byron School."
25. Miles, "Federal Lawsuit Filed Against Byron School."
26. Alexis Amory, "Muslim Re-Education," *FrontPageMagazine.com,* October 20, 2004.
27. Amory, "Muslim Re-Education."
28. Daniel Pipes, OurJerusalem.com, October 30, 2001.
29. Dave Eberhart, "Bodansky," NewsMax.com, October 5, 2004.
30. Peter Brownfield, "Moderate Muslims Speak Out," Fox News, September 7, 2004.
31. Free Muslim Coalition Against Terrorism, "Muslim Group Takes Responsibility for 9-11: 'We Are So Sorry,'" WorldTribune.com, September 10, 2004.
32. Jeff Jacoby, "Where Is the Muslim Outrage?" *Boston Globe,* September 9, 2004.
33. Neil MacFarquhar, "Muslim Scholars Increasingly Debate Unholy War," *New York Times,* December 10, 2004.

3 Alien Invasion

1. Juan A. Lozano, "Federal Officers Sentenced for Not Helping Injured Immigrant," Associated Press, February 3, 2004.
2. Donald L. Barlett and James B. Steele, "Who Left the Door Open?" *Time,* September 20, 2004.
3. From Dover, Delaware, to where I live in the San Francisco Bay area, America is 2,700 miles wide. One mile is 5,280 feet or 63,360 inches. Allowing an average of thirty inches at the shoulders per person, 2,112 people would stand side-by-side per mile. That figure multiplied by 2,700 miles equals 5.7 million people standing coast-to-coast.
4. Barlett and Steele, "Who Left the Door Open?"
5. Bill Gertz, "Chechen Terrorists Probed," *Washington Times,* October 13, 2004.
6. Billy House and Dennis Wagner, "Arizona Was Al-Qaida Hotbed," *Arizona Republic,* July 23, 2004.
7. House and Wagner, "Arizona Was Al-Qaida Hotbed."

8. President Bush, White House Press Release based upon a radio address to the nation, May 5, 2001, http://www.whitehouse.gov/news/releases/2001/05/20010505-1.html.

9. President Ronald Reagan, The President's News Conference, East Room of the White House, June 14, 1984.

10. "Chaos Along the Border," *Washington Times,* October 6, 2002.

11. "Chaos Along the Border," *Washington Times.*

12. "Chaos Along the Border," *Washington Times*

13. Barlett and Steele, "Who Left the Door Open?"

14. Barlett and Steele, "Who Left the Door Open?"

15. William Finn Bennett, "Staffing Shortage Hits Border Patrol," *North County (California) Times,* September 7, 2004.

16. Lisa Myers, "Busted Budgets on the Border," NBC News, July 26, 2004.

17. Ellen Nakashima, "With Gay Pride Observances, a Balancing Act," *Washington Post,* June 12, 2002.

18. Myers, "Busted Budgets on the Border."

19. Myers, "Busted Budgets on the Border."

20. Frosty Wooldridge, "Illegal Alien Driver's License Insanity," NewsMax.com, October 14, 2004.

21. Emma Perez-Trevino, "Potential Terrorists Released Due to Lack of Jail Space, Congressman Says," *Brownsville Herald,* July 23, 2004.

22. Zell Miller, *A National Party No More* (Atlanta: Stroud and Hall, 2003), 157.

23. Miller, 157.

24. John L. Martin, Ira Mehlman, and Alison Green, "State of Insecurity: How State and Local Immigration Policies Are Undermining Homeland Security," FairUS.org, http://www.fairus.org/news/NewsPrint.cfm?ID=1626&c=55.

25. Roy Beck, executive director of NumbersUSA.com, testifying before the U.S. Congress, May 15, 2001.

26. "Solutions: A National Perspective," IllegalAliens.us, http://illegalaliens.us/solutions.htm.

27. Miller, 157.

28. Barlett and Steele, "Who Left the Door Open?"

29. Jerry Seper, "Mexican Ambulances Bring Patients Unable to Pay into U.S.," *Washington Times,* December 12, 2002.

30. Seper, "Mexican Ambulances Bring Patients Unable to Pay into U.S."

31. Haley Nolde, "Border Hospitals on the Brink," MotherJones.com, June 21, 2000.

32. Nolde, "Border Hospitals on the Brink."

33. "The High Cost of Cheap Labor: Illegal Immigration and the Federal Budget," Center for Immigration Studies, August 2004, http://www.cis.org/articles/2004/fiscalexec.html.

34. Michael Doyle, "Hospitals Battle Illegal Immigration Bill," Sacramento Bee, May 14, 2004; "Bankrupt Hospital Serving Hispanic Immigrants Closing," Associated

Press, August 16, 2004; Jon E. Dougherty, *Illegals: The Imminent Threat Posed by Our Unsecured U.S.-Mexico Border* (Nashville: WND Books, 2004), 74–75.

35. "Chaos Along the Border," *Washington Times.*
36. Dan Marries, "American Taxpayers Funding Health Care in Mexico," KOLD-TV, October 10, 2004, http://www.kold.com/global/story.asp?s=2416643.
37. Dick Gephardt, Iowa Brown and Black Presidential Forum, January 11, 2004.
38. DREAM Act position paper of the National Latino Arts, Education, and Media Institute, http://www.nclr.org/content/policy/detail/1221.
39. "The Estimated Cost of Illegal Immigration," Federation for American Immigration Reform policy paper, updated February 2004.
40. "Anchor Babies: The Children of Illegal Aliens," Federation for American Immigration Reform policy paper, updated June 2004, http://www.fairus.org/ImmigrationIssueCenters/ImmigrationIssueCenters.cfm?ID=1190&c=13.
41. "Border Inspectors Find Girl Sealed in Piñata," Associated Press, November 12, 2004.
42. Dana Wilkie, "Whose Problems Are They?" *California Journal,* July 1, 2003.
43. "The High Cost of Cheap Labor: Illegal Immigration and the Federal Budget," August 2004.
44. Carol Moseley-Braun, Democratic Primary Debate, Albuquerque, New Mexico, September 4, 2003.
45. Wooldridge, "Illegal Alien Driver's License Insanity."
46. Michael Vasquez and Gary Fineout, "Governor Endorses Illegal Alien Driving Bill," *Miami Herald,* April 6, 2004.
47. Jeff Lungren and Terry Shawn, "Sensenbrenner: GAO Report Finds Millions of Consular ID Cards Issued by Foreign Governments," *U.S. Newswire,* September 28, 2004.
48. Lungren and Shawn, "Sensenbrenner."
49. Allan Wall, "Memo from Mexico: Good News and Bad News on the Matricula Consular," Vdare.com, May 23, 2003.
50. Allan Wall, "Separate but Superior—Illegal Aliens Emerging as legally-Privileged Class," Vdare.com, August 14, 2004.
51. Art Moore, "Is Mexico Reconquering U.S. Southwest? Illegal Immigration Fueling Aims of Hispanic Radicals," WorldNetDaily.com, January 4, 2002.
52. Barlett and Steele, "Who Left the Door Open?"
53. Barlett and Steele, "Who Left the Door Open?"
54. "US and Mexico Aagree Immigrant Plan," BBC News, August 10, 2001.
55. Dick Gephardt, Fox News, November 17, 2001.
56. Wesley Clark, "Immigration," Q&A, Associated Press, January 25, 2004.
57. "WildAid Congratulates USFWS & Ice and Calls Upon Congress to Put More Resources Into USFWS," PRNewswire, December 20, 2004.

58. Chris Hawley, "Mexico Publishes Guide to Assist Border Crossers," *AZCentral.com,* January 1, 2005.
59. Hawley, "Mexico Publishes Guide to Assist Border Crossers."
60. U.S. Bureau of Justice Statistics, http://www.ojp.usdoj.gov/bjs/pub/press/p02pr.htm.
61. Dana Wilkie, "Just Whose Problems Are They?" *California Journal,* July 1, 2003.
62. Wilkie, "Just Whose Problems Are They?"
63. "The High Cost of Cheap Labor: Illegal Immigration and the Federal Budget," Center for Immigration Studies.
64. "Operation Wetback," Handbook of Texas Online, a publication of the University of Texas at Austin, http://www.tsha.utexas.edu/handbook/online/articles/view/OO/pqo1.html.
65. Department of Energy, Energy Information Agency statistics as of January 2004.
66. Department of Energy, Energy Information Agency, http://www.eia.doe.gov/emeu/cabs/mexico.html.

4 Traders vs. Traitors

1. Jerry Hirsch, "Mexican Avocados to Return Despite State Growers' Fears," *Los Angeles Times,* December 2, 2004.
2. Jerry Seper, "Congressmen Urge Bush to Drop Guest-worker Plan," *Washington Times,* November 17, 2004.
3. "Why Intelligence Bill Is Failing in Congress," WorldNetDaily.com, December 5, 2004.
4. "Why Intelligence Bill Is Failing in Congress," WorldNetDaily.com.
5. Carl Limbacher, "9/11 Report Urges Driver's License Reform," NewsMax.com, December 7, 2004.
6. David Crary, "PETA Campaign Pitches Fish as Smart," Associated Press, November 16, 2004.
7. Crary, "PETA Campaign Pitches Fish as Smart."
8. "PETA Urges Jimmy Carter: Stop Fishing," WorldNetDaily.com, January 4, 2005.
9. David Hurwitz, "History of Vegetarianism: Benjamin Franklin," International Vegetarian Union, available online at: http://www.ivu.org/history/northam18/franklin.html.
10. "Bill Would Force Hiring of Cross-dressers," WorldNetDaily.com, April 21, 2003.
11. Clyde Wayne Crews Jr., "Ten Thousand Commandments," Cato Institute, 2003.
12. Brian Headd, "Business Success: Factors Leading to Surviving and Closing Successfully," Center for Economic Studies, U.S. Bureau of the Census, Working Paper #CES-WP-01-01, January 2001.
13. Susan E. Dudley, "A Regulated Day in the Life," *Regulation,* Summer 2004.
14. Crews, "Ten Thousand Commandments."
15. Crews, "Ten Thousand Commandments."
16. Walter Olson, "Occupational Hazards," *Reason,* May 1997.

17. Tillinghast-Towers Perrin, U.S. Tort Costs: 2002 Update, Trends and Findings on the Costs of the U.S. Tort System, February 19, 2003.
18. Tillinghast-Towers Perrin.
19. "Trial Lawyers, Inc.: A Report on the Lawsuit Industry in America 2003," Center for Legal Policy at the Manhattan Institute.
20. "Trial Lawyers, Inc."
21. Deroy Murdock, "Criminals Who Sue," *American Enterprise,* June 1, 2003.
22. "Short News and Commentary," American Enterprise Online, June 2003, available at: http://www.taemag.com/issues/articleid.17337/article_detail.asp.
23. "Trial Lawyers, Inc."
24. Joseph A. Slobodzian, "City Abruptly Settles Suicide-prevention Suit for $3.5 Million," *Inquirer,* November 23, 2004.
25. Adam Liptak and Michael Moss, "In Trial Work, Edwards Left a Trademark," *New York Times,* January 31, 2004.
26. Matt Pinnell, "Hunt for the Frivolous Lawsuit: How Trial Lawyers Are Targeting Auto Dealers, and Making Off with Millions," *FastTrack,* The American International Automobile Dealers Association, September 28, 2004.
27. David Boldt, "Wretched Excesses of Liability Lawsuits," *Philadelphia Inquirer,* November 29, 1999.
28. Bill Mears, "Supreme Court Throws Out Large Jury Award Involving Automaker," CNN.com, May 19, 2003.
29. "Trial Lawyers, Inc."
30. "Modern Plague: Trial Laywers, Inc." The Center for Consumer Freedom, September 24, 2003.
31. Bruce Bartlett, "Burden of Proof," *National Review Online,*·December 15, 2003.

5   Arafat, Clinton, Kinsey: Sympathy for the Devil

1. "Arafat Skimmed $2 Million a Month from the Gas Trade," DrudgeReport.com, November 14, 2004.
2. Aaron Klein, "New York Times Gushes over Arafat: Long Tribute Blames Israel for Terrorism, Calls Dead Leader 'Enigmatic Statesman.'" WorldNetDaily.com, November 12, 2004.
3. Klein, "New York Times Gushes over Arafat."
4. Andrea Stone, "Arab World Mourns Death of Arafat," *USA Today,* November 11, 2004.
5. Carl Limbacher, "Chirac Praises Terrorist Arafat; Australia's Howard Gets It Right," NewsMax.com, November 11, 2004.
6. Limbacher, "Chirac Praises."
7. Limbacher, "Chirac Praises."
8. Limbacher, "Chirac Praises."
9. "Jihad for Kids," http://radiobergen.org/palestine/jihad.html. See also, David

Bedein, "Your Taxes for PLO Propaganda," FrontPageMagazine.com, October 29, 2003.

10. Patrick Goodenough, "From the Mouths of Babes," CNS Jerusalem Bureau Chief, March 23, 1999.

11. Goodenough, "From the Mouths of Babes."

12. Goodenough, "From the Mouths of Babes."

13. Goodenough, "From the Mouths of Babes."

14. Limbacher, "Chirac Praises."

15. Carl Limbacher, "Arafat & Friends in Their Own Words," NewsMax.com, November 11, 2004.

16. David Huntwork, "Yasser Arafat: The Life and Death of a Monster," MensNewsDaily.com, November 13, 2004.

17. Joel Leyden, "Arafat Fearing Israel Abandons Fatah Terrorists," Israel News Agency, April 23, 2004.

18. Leyden, "Arafat Fearing Israel Abandons Fatah Terrorists."

19. Huntwork, "Yasser Arafat."

20. Jeff Jacoby, "Arafat the Monster," *Boston Globe,* November 11, 2004.

21. "Yasser Arafat, 1929–2004," HonestReporting.com, November 11, 2004.

22. "Outing Arafat," WorldNetDaily.com, September 22, 2003.

23. "Selling Sex in the U.S.A.," WorldNetDaily.com, November 12, 2004.

24. "Selling Sex in the U.S.A.," WorldNetDaily.com.

25. Susan P. Brinkman, "Sordid 'Science': The Children of Table 34," *Catholic Standard & Times,* available at http://www.drjudithreisman.com/3of7.htm.

26. Brinkman, "Sordid 'Science.'"

27. "Selling Sex in the U.S.A.," WorldNetDaily.com.

28. James H. Jones, *Alfred C. Kinsey: A Public/Private Life* (New York: W.W. Norton, 1997).

29. "Former President Criticizes Clinton's Last-minute Pardons," Associated Press, February 21, 2001.

30. Niles Lathem, "City, Fed Probes Eye Pardongate Billionaire as a 'Major Player' in Saddam's Scam," *New York Post,* December 13, 2004.

31. Fr. Michael Reilly, "Clinton Legacy Poll: It's All About Sex," NewsMax.com, November 26, 2004.

32. "The Clinton Legacy," *Progressive Review,* http://prorev.com/legacy.htm.

33. Marc Morano, "Christianity Harmful to Animals," CNSNews.com, July 1, 2002.

34. Marvin Olasky, "Blue-State Philosopher," *World,* November 27, 2004.

35. Morano, "Christianity Harmful to Animals."

36. Susan Sontag, "Talk of the Town," *New Yorker,* September 24, 2001.

37. Sontag, "Talk of the Town."

38. Susan Sontag, "Real Battles and Empty Metaphors," *New York Times,* September 10, 2002.

39. Claudia Parsons, "Susan Sontag Dies at 71," Reuters, December 28, 2004.
40. Carol Memmott, "Susan Sontag: Always One to Speak Up," *USA Today,* December 28, 2004.

6   Head of the Snake: The ACLU

1. Murdo MacLeod, "Van Gogh Murder Backlash Begins," Scotsman.com, November 8, 2004.
2. MacLeod, "Van Gogh Murder Backlash Begins."
3. Lisa Porteus, "Officials Warn of Summer Terror Threats," Fox News, July 8, 2004.
4. Kerry Sheridan, "State-of-the-Art Security to Make Debut at Republican Convention," Voice of America, August 26, 2004.
5. Live NY1-TV news broadcast, August 26, 2004.
6. Dana Bash, "Bush Pushes $15 Billion for AIDS Fight," CNN.com, April 30, 2003.
7. John J. Tierney, "The Supporter of Castro's Cuba Who Organized Sunday's Anti-Bush March Through New York City," Capital Research Center, August 30, 2004, http://www.capitalresearch.org/news/news.asp?ID=243.
8. Tierney, "The Supporter of Castro's Cuba Who Organized Sunday's Anti-Bush March Through New York City."
9. Tierney, "The Supporter of Castro's Cuba Who Organized Sunday's Anti-Bush March Through New York City."
10. Tierney, "The Supporter of Castro's Cuba Who Organized Sunday's Anti-Bush March Through New York City."
11. "Pro-Troop Organization Set to Fight Back Against 'Blame America' Crowd," NewsMax.com, August 18, 2004.
12. "Ignorant Protestors," *Pittsburgh Tribune-Review,* September 12, 2004.
13. Louis Bulow, "Gates to Hell: Nazi KZ Camps," http://www.deathcamps.info.
14. David Remnick, "Leaders & Revolutionaries: V.I. Lenin," *Time,* http://www.time.com/time/time100/leaders/profile/lenin.html.
15. "Case Study: Stalin's Purges," Gendercide.org, http://www.gendercide.org/case_stalin.html.
16. Kristen Philipkoski, "Eco-terror Cited as Top Threat," *Wired News,* June 16, 2004.
17. Philipkoski, "Eco-terror Cited as Top Threat."
18. "Terrorism Q & A," Council on Foreign Relations, Web site, accessed September 15, 2004, http://cfrterrorism.org/terrorism/types_print.html.
19. Nonprofitjobs.org, http://www.nonprofitjobs.org/jdetail.cfm?jid=12555.
20. Nonprofitjobs.org, http://www.nonprofitjobs.org/jdetail.cfm?jid=12555.
21. ACLU statistic, available at: http://www.aclu.org.
22. ACLU statistic, available at: http://www.aclu.org.
23. ACLU Press Release, October 22, 1997, "NJ Court Grants Joint Adoption to Gay Couple."

ENDNOTES

7   The Red and the Blue

1. Richard E. Cohen, *National Journal*/Govexec.com, February 27, 2004.
2. Brit Hume, "Putting Words in His Mouth?" FoxNews.com, January 18, 2005.
3. Press Release, "First Federal Lawsuit Filed to Overturn a State Marriage Amendment," The Alliance for Marriage, http://www.allianceformarriage.org/site/News2?page=NewsArticle&id=5550.
4. Senator Edward M. Kennedy, "Defending Marriage for Gay Couples," WashingtonBlade.com, July 23, 2004.
5. Alexa Baracaia, "Elton Changes Tune over Bush," *The Evening Standard,* December 6, 2004.
6. Carl Limbacher, "White House: Kerry Should Apologize for Filthy Fund-Raiser," NewsMax.com, July 9, 2004.
7. "Carlson Equates Goldberg's Sexual Crudity with Limbaugh's Quips," Media Research Center, July 12, 2004.
8. Jennifer King, "Whoopie Cushion," GOPUSA.com, July 19, 2004.
9. Dana Milbank, "Do You Hear What I Hear?" WashingtonPost.com, August 24, 2004.
10. Limbacher, "White House: Kerry Should Apologize for Filthy Fund-Raiser,"
11. Senator Edward M. Kennedy, "A Democratic Blueprint for America's Future," Address given at the National Press Club, January 12, 2005.
12. Gene Edward Veith, "Taliban West?" *World,* December 25, 2004.
13. Michael Jonas, "Sen. Clinton Urges Use of Faith-based Initiatives," *Boston Globe,* January 20, 2005.
14. Peter LaBarbera, "Portland, Oregon, Mayor Proclaims 'Leather Pride Week' for Sexual Sadists," CultureandFamilyInstitute.org, September 11, 2002.
15. Lawrence Wallack, "News: Mayor Vera Katz to Join PSU," Press Release #04-161, PSU College of Urban and Public Affairs, December 10, 2004.
16. Hillary Clinton, "Gays Deserve Domestic Partnership Benefits," CNN.com, February 11, 2000.
17. John Kerry, "Transcript of John Kerry's Concession Speech," *The New York Times,* November 3, 2004.
18. Maureen Dowd, "Rove's Revenge," *The New York Times,* November 7, 2004.
19. Tom Hess and Karla Dial, "Year of the Values Voter," *Citizen,* January 2005.
20. Dowd, "Rove's Revenge."
21. "What Do We Do Now?" Salon.com, 4 November 2004.
22. Timothy Heritage, "Four More Years of Bush Makes the World Anxious," Reuters, January 19, 2005.
23. Kurt A. Gardinier, "Clinton Calls for Change to 22nd Amendment," Press release, TermLimits.org, May 29, 2003.
24. Stephen Dinan, "Hill Cool to Clinton's President-term Idea," *Washington Times,* June 5, 2003.

25. James Harding, "Soros Group Raises Stakes in Battle with US Neo-cons," *Financial Times,* FT.com, January 11, 2005.
26. "The La Follette Progressives," U-S-History.com.
27. Kennedy, "A Democratic Blueprint for America's Future."
28. Kennedy, "A Democratic Blueprint for America's Future."
29. Kennedy, "A Democratic Blueprint for America's Future."

PAUL REVERE SOCIETY
MISSION STATEMENT

⌒

MICHAEL SAVAGE founded the Paul Revere Society (PRS). With a crisis of leadership threatening the United States, PRS stands for the reassertion of our borders, our language, and our culture.

Some say that the borders are arbitrary, English is only one of many languages in our new "Multicultural America," and that we share no common history or values. We believe in the Sovereignty of our Nation. That English is our national "glue." And that we all do share in the pillars of the *Bible,* the *U.S. Constitution,* and the *Bill of Rights.* These documents and what they stand for are our common cultural heritage.

The Paul Revere Society will assert the values inherent in these pillars of freedom. We will seek to educate the citizenry about our nation's freedoms.

SPONSOR
THE
PAUL REVERE SOCIETY!

A Non-Profit 501(c)(3) Organization
Federal Tax Exempt # 91-1786633

Your sponsorship will help make your voice heard,
By helping our educational organization make our voice heard
To the people who need to hear our message concerning this
Great Nation's Borders, Language, and Culture.

Your Sponsorship includes our Generous Package of
Free Merchandise, Not Available in Stores, which has a Value that
Exceeds the Sponsorship Fee, along with Your Numbered
Unique Sponsorship Card.

COMPLETE THE FOLLOWING FORM.
SUBMISSION INSTRUCTIONS FOLLOW.

THE PAUL REVERE SOCIETY, INC. SPONSORSHIP FORM

Name

Address:

City: State: Zip:

Optional: Telephone (Home)   (Work)   (Mobile)

Payment Method (Circle one):

Money Order   Check   Credit Card

I authorize The Paul Revere Society to charge the following amount to my credit card:

(Circle your choice, please)
One-Year Sponsorship: $40; Two-Year Sponsorship: $70; Contribution: $_____

TWO-YEAR SPONSORSHIP ($70) INCLUDES:

- Official Paul Revere Society Sponsorship Card
- Discounts and Advance Notice for Future Events
- Free SAVAGE NATION Baseball Cap, Navy Blue with Embroidered Lettering ($24.95 Value, Made in USA)
- ADDED BONUS: Double CD Set, THE BEST OF THE SAVAGE NATION ($24.95 Value, Made in USA)
- The Honor of Helping to Build America's Premier Educational Organization

ONE-YEAR SPONSORSHIP ($40) INCLUDES:

- Official Paul Revere Society Sponsorship Card
- Discounts and Advance Notice for Future Events
- Free SAVAGE NATION Baseball Cap, Navy Blue with Embroidered Lettering ($24.95 Value, Made in USA)
- The Honor of Helping to Build America's Premier Educational Organization

HELP US GROW! I WANT TO CONTRIBUTE AN ADDITIONAL:
(Circle your choice) $100 $250 $500 $1,000   OTHER: _____

CREDIT CARD INFORMATION:
(Note: We utilize the secured Bank of America e-commerce online division for your protection. We will never share your personal information with anyone.)

NAME ON CARD
ADDRESS ON CARD
TYPE OF CARD: (Circle one)   VISA   MASTERCARD
CARD NUMBER
EXPIRATION DATE ON CARD

I authorize the Paul Revere Society to charge my credit card as follows (Circle one):
One Year Sponsorship $40; Two Year Sponsorship $70; Contribution $_____

Complete this form and send it with your payment (check, cash, money order, or credit card) to:
THE PAUL REVERE SOCIETY, INC
150 SHORELINE HIGHWAY, BLDG "E"
MILL VALLEY, CA 94941

TELEPHONE: 415-339-9377
THIS FORM MAY BE FAXED TO: 415-339-9383
(All information submitted will never be sold or shared with any other entity.)

NELSON CURRENT

N elson Current, the political imprint of Thomas Nelson, Inc., publishes probing, engaging, thought-provoking titles that explore the political landscape with audacity and integrity. With a stable of news-making writers including both veteran journalists and rising stars, as well as *New York Times* best-selling authors such as Michael Savage, Nelson Current has quickly established itself as a clear leader in the ever-expanding genre of political publishing.

Check out other provocative, relevant, and timely books at NelsonCurrent.com.

THE POLITICAL ZOO
By Michael Savage
1-59555-042-9

Savage's funniest, most biting book yet takes readers through the zoo of political debate, comparing today's most prominent politicians and pundits to various species of animals. From junkyard dog James Carville to the Reverend Al Sharkton (who can "smell a single drop of racial tension from miles away, but is easily spotted by its dorsal fin of hair"), from the toothless flip-flopping dolphin John Kerry ("not even Eggo has as many waffles") to dwarf elephant George W. Bush (also known as *Dumbo disappointus*), *The Political Zoo* is a riotous tour through the political-animal kingdom that gives Savage treatment to today's cultural rats, worms, and snakes.

Donkey Cons
*Sex, Crime, and Violence in the
Democratic Party*
By Lynn Vincent and Robert Stacy McCain
1-59555-024-0

From bribery, kickbacks, and sex scandals to espionage, terrorism, and rape, *Donkey Cons* chronicles, for the first time, the panorama of Democratic crime and corruption, showing how the party developed a "criminal personality" that hatches policies hazardous to the constitutional rights of every American. Thoroughly researched, using outrageous anecdotes and intimate details, *Donkey Cons* shows that the serial corruption of the Clinton presidency wasn't an anomaly, but the logical legacy of the modern Democratic ethos. It's like author McCain says, "The Democratic Party is like the Gambino mob with matching federal funds."

Muzzled
*From T-Ball to Terrorism—True Stories that
Should Be Fiction*
By Michael Smerconish
1-59555-050-X

This brazen, furiously funny book is the antidote to today's poison of political correctness. With humor and chutzpah, attorney, commentator, and popular radio host Michael Smerconish takes on today's oversensitive culture with a collection of entertaining, outlandish tales about PC gone wild—stories that are hilarious, horrifying, and unbelievably true—and shows through these absurdities that today's atmosphere of censorship and multiculturalism is paving the way for serious threats to our cultural identity and national security: "It's one thing for the forces of political correctness to muzzle our day-to-day lives here at home in the US, quite another when that same cancer metastasizes into the war on terror."

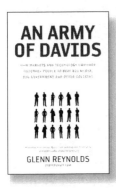

AN ARMY OF DAVIDS
*How Markets and Technology Empower
Ordinary People to Beat Big Media, Big
Government, and Other Goliaths*
By Glenn Reynolds
1-59555-054-2

In *Army of Davids*, author Glenn Reynolds, the man behind the immensely popular Instapundit.com, provides an in-depth, big-picture point-of-view for a world where the small guys matter more and more. Reynolds explores the birth and growth of the individual's surprisingly strong influence in arts and entertainment, anti-terrorism, nanotech and space research, and much more. There was a time in the not-too-distant past when large companies and powerful governments reigned supreme over the little guy. But new technologies are empowering individuals like never before, and the Davids of the world—the amateur journalists, musicians, and small businessmen and women—are, as Reynolds shows, suddenly making a huge economic and social impact.

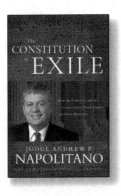

THE CONSTITUTION IN EXILE
*How the Congress and the Courts Stole Your
Freedom and Your Property*
By Judge Andrew P. Napolitano
1-59555-030-5

The Constitution permits Congress to regulate interstate commerce—which, as Fox News analyst Judge Napolitano proves in this book, has opened the floodgates of federal abuse, as the government trounces on state and individual rights, expanding its reach far beyond what the Framers intended. With no-nonsense clarity, Napolitano shows that Congress has "purchased" regulations by bribing states—giving huge amounts of taxpayer dollars on condition that states enact regulations of human behavior that Congress prefers but cannot legislate. Tapping into the intense distrust of activist judges, Napolitano also explains how the Supreme Court has devised historically inaccurate, logically inconsistent, and even laughable justifications to approve what Congress has done.

Made in the USA
San Bernardino, CA
24 July 2017